THE
Overcomers

Discovering Hope in the Book of Revelation

SECOND EDITION

THE Overcomers

Discovering Hope in the Book of Revelation

SECOND EDITION

Chuck Colclasure

Foreword by D. James Kennedy

JORDAN*publishing*

Rights and Permissions
Jordan Publishing
P.O. Box 3043
Anderson, Indiana 46018-3043

info@jordanpublishing.net

Scripture quotations are from the New American Standard Bible, © The Lockman Foundation 1960, 1962, 1963, 1968, 1971, 1972, 1973, 1975, and are used by permission.

COVER PHOTO: The photograph on this book's cover is a view of the Aegean Sea as seen from the cave on the Island of Patmos, where it is believed John lived in exile during his writing of the book of Revelation.

Cover design by Mary J. Jaracz Design

Cover photo by Georgethefourth/Shutterstock, used by permission.

Paperback   ISBN 978-1-891314-17-9
ePub   ISBN 978-1-891314-18-6

Printed in the United States of America

To
Mom Smith, Jack, Glenn, and Rick
who have met and overcome the last enemy
and to
Lauren
who has just begun the fight

CONTENTS

FOREWORD

Chuck Colclasure has performed a valuable service to the church by writing a work on the Book of Revelation from a pastoral viewpoint. He has recognized that the book was originally written to be an encouragement to the churches.

The Book of Revelation pronounces a blessing upon those who read it, and yet many people have been discouraged from doing so by the complexity of its symbolism and the controversy concerning its eschatology.

Reverend Colclasure has tried to cut through these problems and to show the readers the many spiritual truths and lessons that are contained within the book. They provide strength and encouragement for the Christian in his daily battle with the forces of evil.

Those who are looking for material to fill their previously constructed theological or eschatological cubbyholes may be disappointed, but the Christian, who is looking for strength for the day . . . for courage for the battle . . . and for hope for tomorrow, will find great reward in the pages of this book, and will have taken a large step toward becoming an *overcomer.*

D. James Kennedy
Founding Pastor
Coral Ridge Presbyterian Church
Fort Lauderdale, Florida

PREFACE TO

THE SECOND EDITION

As I write these words, the globe seems to be experiencing a social and economic shutdown. The coronavirus, which surfaced in China in late 2019, has now spread to nearly two hundred countries worldwide, having infected almost three million people and bringing about some three hundred thousand deaths. The World Health Organization has declared the situation a global pandemic.

Around the world, people are instructed to "shelter in place," permitted to leave their homes for only the most essential reasons. Families, friends, and neighbors are restricted from spending time together, and even hugs are forbidden. Literally, what in the world is going on?

Is this present worldwide pandemic the fulfillment of biblical prophesies? Have we finally seen the arrival of the "pale horse" of Revelation 6, who brings with him "Death" and "Hades?"

Perhaps. But what would you have thought if you were a first-century Christian experiencing persecution and even death at the command of the evil emperors of the Roman Empire? What would your belief have been if you were among the 200 million people afflicted with and killed by the Black Death in Europe and North Africa in the 1300s? Surely that was "the pale horse," wasn't it? Or was it the devastation of two World Wars and countless other deadly conflicts throughout the ages?

The point, as will be elucidated in this book, is that humanity has always been afflicted with terrors in this world. You are the descendent of people who endured and survived war, plague, and pestilence. And you well may be called to endure the same.

Does this mean that somehow God has lost control, that evil has finally gained the upper hand, and that our faith and our hopes are dashed, at last? I think the answer found in the Book of Revelation is: "Not at all!"

Rather than being intended to frighten and horrify us with its startling imagery, the true purpose of the Book of Revelation is to provide hope, comfort, and encouragement to those who continue to trust in God, even during the most difficult of times—perhaps especially during the most difficult of times.

This has made the Book of Revelation relevant to all generations of Christians, from the original readers and hearers of the words of this book in the first century until today, and beyond.

I hope your reading of *The Overcomers*, and more importantly of the Book of Revelation itself, will fulfill its purpose in your heart, your mind, and your experience, by providing you with hope, comfort, and encouragement as you walk the path of faith.

Chuck Colclasure
San Diego
May 2020

ACKNOWLEDGMENTS

Many brothers and sisters have been used by God to minister to me as this book moved toward completion. Unfortunately, only a few can be specially mentioned here.

Thanks to my students in the Revelation classes I have taught at the Greenhouse and at Coral Ridge Presbyterian Church, for their encouraging me to begin this project.

Thanks to Bill Warder, who made me get things out of my head and on to paper.

Thanks to Greg and Julie Baldwin and my other friends on Hilton Head Island, for providing me with a place to think and write.

Thanks to my secretary, Kay Senderling, for her excellence and patience in correcting and typing a mountain of manuscripts.

Thanks to Jim Kennedy, for his willingness and availability to write the foreword to this book.

INTRODUCTION

When you think of the portions of Scripture which have proven especially helpful to you, those which have counseled you through trials and lifted your heart from disappointment, which passages come to mind? The Psalms? The Gospel of John? The Epistles?

If you've been bothered with worry, perhaps Paul's admonition has relieved your anxieties: "Be anxious for nothing, but in everything by prayer and supplication with thanksgiving let your requests be made known to God" (Phil. 4:6).

Or maybe you've had trouble with temptation, and you recalled that "no temptation has overtaken you but such as is common to man; and God is faithful, who will not allow you to be tempted beyond what you are able..." (1 Cor. 10:13).

Most of us know verses like these which have become special to us; sometimes whole chapters or books of the Bible seem to be speaking specifically and pointedly to our current needs.

But I wonder if you've ever thought of the *Book of Revelation* as being one of those especially comforting and encouraging books. I never had. In fact, the only emotional surge I got from the Revelation was one of *fear.* Instead of comforting me, those bizarre visions scared me half to death.

I think the reason the Revelation didn't administer hope and encouragement to me in my daily life was this: The teaching I had received concerning the book relegated its meaning solely to some period of frightening global disruption in the future, far removed from my needs in the here and now. Therefore, the Revelation seemed unrelated to my real life—interesting, but frightening and irrelevant.

My purpose in writing this book is to help you understand and apply the spiritual principles unveiled in the Revelation and to help you enjoy its benefits and blessings today. Together, we will look at the book devotionally—inspirationally.

Remember that the Revelation is primarily a pastoral book, written by an apostolic pastor of several churches to his flocks. His theme was to urge God's people to overcome the world. It was not intended to frighten and perplex them but to provide for their encouragement, warning, exhortation, and comfort. Just as the book was full of exciting meaning for those late first-century believers to whom it was originally written, so it can be for you.

If you've shied away from the Revelation before, let me introduce you to a most personal and practical book which can be of immense spiritual value to you in your "here and now" walk with Christ. *Blessed* are all who read and heed the words of this prophecy.*   1:3

---

*As you read the pages of this volume, you will see margin references to passages from the Revelation. These verse listings indicate the portions of the Revelation discussed on each page.

This book is intended to be read alongside an open Bible—I hope you will study it in that way. May God grant you a heart of understanding that through His Word you will discover a clearer perception of His will and His ways in your life.

1. Finders, Keepers

What are you looking for in life? All the gusto you can get? A Coke and a smile? A piece of the rock? A happy marriage, two kids, and a house in the suburbs?

If the images of security and success that the world projects to us are true, all of the above are proper goals. You and I will be appropriately overjoyed with the discovery of an oven cleaner which bubbles away grime while we play a set of tennis.

But you know that's not the way it really is. Each of us wants more than those things out of life. We need more. What all of us really require, what we're really looking for, is something certain, something absolute, something that won't change even when we and the rest of the world do. We are looking for the kind of things that ultimately only God can give.

Now most people won't come out and say it like that, but nevertheless men and women today seek and need the securities and certainties that only the living God can provide.

Admittedly they often look for these things in some strange places—in fact, most folks look for them everywhere except in God. It's then that those of us who have found Him (or rather, have been found by Him) need to help them look beyond their previous boundaries—even when they don't seem to want any help.

All this searching might tend to get frustrating, except for some very good news—news that God Himself gives us. He has told us that he who really seeks will find, and that what we find, we can keep (see Matt.

7:7,8). That makes it pretty important that we look for the right answer: the true and living God.

But how do we know who He is so that we can look for Him? How can we tell if we've truly found Him? Those are good questions. He has taken care of them by going to the trouble of revealing Himself, in a Book and in a human Person. Those who refuse to go to that Book and to that Person—through which God the Father tells us who He is—will obviously have a much more difficult time finding Him. In fact, they might find an imitation god and think it is the real thing, all because they have refused God's true revelation in the Bible and in Jesus Christ.

Revelation: Who Needs It?

The concept of revelation is extremely important for us to understand. The Greek word which is translated *revelation* is used in two ways in the Bible. Its general meaning is "the uncovering of something which has been previously hidden." After the Fall, God revealed Himself to only a select group of people—first to men like Abraham and Job; then to the Jews through the Law and the Prophets, and finally, through His Son, Jesus the Christ. It was necessary for God to tell us how He may be found because our sin had separated us from Him. Without the truth which is revealed in the Scriptures, we would have no idea about the true way to heaven. We would think up our own way of trying to get there, and it would surely be wrong. As the Proverb says, "There is a way which seems right to a man, but its end is the way of death" (14:12). In this sense of the word, revelation is absolutely essential for everyone who really seeks the true God.

But there is another way in which the Scripture uses the word *revelation:* as the title of the last book of the Bible. This final book, written by the apostle John, reveals some things which most of the other books of the Bible don't deal with. It tells us of the spiritual history of the world subsequent to the life, death, and resurrection of Jesus. It talks about the end of the world, marked by the return of Christ, the bodily resurrection of His people, and His final judgment of the world. Other books of the Bible touch on these things, but the Book of Revelation is devoted to them.

If the Book of Revelation offers us God's word on these fascinating subjects, why is it that many of God's people throughout history have shied away from its study? And why, on the other hand, do some modern Christians get so wrapped up in this book that they seem to lose proper balance in their understanding of the rest of the Bible?

The frustration many Christians feel with the Revelation arises from the fact that they have been frightened by the bizarre symbols in the book: seven-headed beasts, demonic locusts, the moon turning to blood, and so on. As one woman said to me, "I'd rather be ignorant than scared to death!" So she had neglected Revelation.

Other believers have experienced an opposite frustration. They have limited themselves to astroprojecting the meaning of the Revelation into some future aeon and transmitting the truths of the book only into that yet unhappened age. Thus the blessing of the Revelation's teaching falls always beyond their grasp, always being out there somewhere in a future age.

I want you to see that you can take the words our Savior spoke to John and apply their comforts and warnings to your life *today*. Your daily hassles, the fears you battle, the uncertainty of your future, all the things that get to you in this age—the message of the Revelation can help you to overcome.

If you and I are to understand the spiritual principles at work in our lives today, both for good and for evil, we must study the Revelation. Although some people are frightened by the language of the book, its purpose is actually to comfort us who trust in the Lord Jesus and to encourage us to remain faithful to Him, whatever the cost.

A Book for All Seasons— And Especially for Today

Because the Revelation is descriptive of spiritual principles which have been at work since the Cross, its words have been encouraging and its study rewarding to believers throughout the history of the church. But few generations have had the opportunities for immediate application of the truths in this book which we enjoy today. Though the spirit of antichrist has been afoot since the first century (see 1 John 2:18), its blinding, evil activity in the minds and hearts of men has never been greater than in our time. If there has ever been a day when the church needed to hear and heed the message of the Book of Revelation, it is today.

I should stress here what I have hinted at above: The Book of Revelation is not about the end of the world *per se*. Its call to us is to trust and obey Jesus Christ, to anticipate His glorious kingdom. It includes several descriptions of the end, but it does so primarily because the end of a story is an essential part of the story. The story of the Revelation is spiritual history, a history which has a beginning, a middle, and an end—all of which are important. But we live in the here and now, and we must discover what God wants us to know about today. The Book of Revelation helps in that discovery.

Let's begin our study by turning to the opening verses of the Revelation's first chapter. Pray that God the Holy Spirit will teach you from His Word, and that He will enable you to know Him and see Him more clearly as a result of your searching for Him in this amazing book of prophecy.

Whose Revelation Is This?

As we have already noted, *revelation* means "the uncovering of something which has been previously hidden." That which is revealed in any revelation is new information about a particular person or subject, information formerly unknown to people. Thus it is only God Himself who can grant a true *revelation*.

This fact should cause us to question the traditional title of the book we are studying. Most editions of the Bible list its title as "The Revelation of St. John" or some such similar appellation. But really, is it John who is being revealed to us? Is the focus of the book concerned with telling us unknown facts about this apostle? Or is he even the ultimate author of the book?

Of course not. Even before beginning our study of the Revelation we know that much. This set of prophecies is revelatory of *Jesus Christ Himself,* of His rule over the nations of the world, and of His coming at the end of the age. These are the previously unknown truths which are opened before us in the pages of this book.

Thus we find that the opening words of the first chapter of this prophetic book provide us with its true title: **1:1** "The Revelation of *Jesus Christ.*" We know, of course, that the apostle John was used by God to pen the words before us, and in that sense the prophecy is his. But at the outset of our investigation into the meaning of the Revelation, we must see that from its beginning to its end, this book reveals to us Jesus and His plans for His people, the church. Have you wanted to know Jesus better? Would you like to understand more fully His ways of working in your life? If so, this book is for you.

Reserved Especially for You:
One Available Blessing

The Revelation opens with a description of a revelatory chain which God uses to communicate the message of this book to you and me today. God the Father gave the Revelation to Jesus, who communicated it by His angel to the apostle John. John "published" the 1:2 book, saw its message spread throughout his world, and now, the message having been preserved through the centuries, he speaks to you and me.

It is absolutely vital for us to remember that the Revelation was originally delivered to our believing brothers and sisters, people like you and me, who lived in Asia Minor (modern Turkey). Most important of all, it was meaningful to them. How can we be sure that they understood the meaning of this book? We know those original readers and hearers grasped the Revelation's meaning because of a unique promise contained in the first chapter: "Blessed is he who reads and those who hear the words of the prophecy, and heed the things which are written in it. . . ." The portion of God's Word which you are about to study is the only book of the Bible which *promises* a blessing to all who read it and heed it. All Scripture is, of course, inspired by God and is profitable to those who conform their lives to it (see 2 Tim. 3:16,17), but the Revelation offers a blessing which is specially mentioned.

To whom is this promise of blessing addressed? To those who "read," "hear," and "heed" the words of this prophecy. Is any historical limitation placed upon that promise? No. Are there any apparent geographical boundaries outside of which the promise of God is null and void? None at all.

From this verse's unqualified promise of blessing we conclude the obvious: The Book of Revelation is not some mysterious and apparently unsolvable puzzle which can be understood only by a handful of believers living at the time of the end of the world. It is instead a book of the Bible which has been understood and applied by believers in the first century, the second century, and throughout the history of the church. Its meaning is relevant for us today as well.

As we are told in the introductory verses of the book, "the time [for the fulfillment of the book's prophecies] is near." The time was near when John wrote those words, and the vitality of the Revelation's message has not dwindled but rather increased with the passing of the centuries.

Address and Signature

In verse 1 John informs us of the source of the visions: It is God Himself who has granted these revelations. But it is the man John who is actually writing the words of the prophecy, and he is writing them specifically for the eyes and ears of people whom he knows and loves. These people were the members of the seven churches of Asia Minor.

Historical accounts reveal that the aged apostle was associated with these ancient churches, serving as an itinerant overseer for them. In this sense the Revelation can be seen to be a pastoral letter from a loving shepherd to his flocks. As such the book contains warnings, rebukes, exhortations, and encouragements meant for those churches. Since the unbelieving world has continued to display the same evil characteristics down through the centuries as it did in the first, and because the promises of Jesus to His people remain true regardless of the era, we will be wise to take them seriously.

The God Who Is Here

As was the custom with many early Christian writers, John begins his communication to the churches with a doxology of praise to the triune God. This particular doxology is unique, however, for it introduces symbolic representations of the persons of the Trinity which are used again in the subsequent visions of the Revelation. It will be well worth our efforts to take a close look at these words of adoration for the Godhead.

What is the most important truth you can know about God? There are several reasonable responses to that question: that He is merciful; that He is just; that He is love; that He offers eternal life to those who hunger after it. Each of these constitutes an appropriate answer to the query. But there is one attribute of God upon which everything else said about Him rests: God is the God "who is". (see Ex. 3:14). He is the God who exists in reality. He is "the God who is here."

This may seem to be a rather obvious point, but it is precisely what the early church needed to be reminded of, and it is also what we need to remember today. God is not some theological projection or some philosophical speculation. He exists unchangingly. He is! And He is active in the affairs of men in this present age, as He was in previous ages, and as He will be in the age to come.

The crucial importance of this point must not be forgotten. The infant church of the first century was a troubled church; it was under attack from the unbelieving world surrounding it. Sometimes when those first Christians prayed for protection and deliverance from persecution, it seemed that the heavens were brass, that God was silent—or perhaps not there at all! But at the beginning of his communication to these seven ancient churches, John reminds them that God *is* there, and that He has a steadfast purpose, though at times unseen, in all that He brings to pass.

There are times in all of our lives when we need to remind ourselves of the fact that God *is* in the here and now. Near the end of 1979, three of my closest Christian friends were tragically killed in a hot air balloon crash. These young men left behind wives, children, and loved ones, and they each had obvious potential for significant service to Christ.

Why did God allow them to die? Did He turn away His head from watching over them? Did He forget that they were His children? Did He move for a few moments to some far corner of the universe, too far away to know what was happening? No, none of those is the case. While I don't know all of the answers to the difficult questions of life and death, I do know this: God is, and He is mindful of His people, of you and me, today.

He is also the One "who was." Jehovah is the God of history. Even before there was such a thing as history, He existed (see Is. 41:4). And as the Creator, He brought the heavens and the earth and time itself into being. As the Sustainer, He has kept all things "running" even up until this present moment. God is the God "who was."

Finally, He is the God "who is to come." He is the One who ordains the future, and the destiny of every thing and every person is under His sovereign control (see Eph. 1:11). All eternity is under His sway, including your eternal hopes and mine. Those who belong to Him need not fear the future, for He has already been there to prepare the way for us. Even when that way seems impassable, we must remember that the future falls to us moment by moment from the One who loves us. Whatever comes upon us is for our ultimate good (see Rom. 8:28). This truth was a welcome reminder to our first century brethren; it should be the same to us.

The Seven-Fold Spirit

Although the Revelation is a book inspired by the Holy Spirit, it does not have a great deal to teach specifically concerning the Holy Spirit. Nevertheless, John has an interesting way of referring to the characteristics of the Holy Spirit, which are called "the seven

Spirits" of God. What does this mysterious phrase mean?

The prophet Isaiah speaks of seven characteristics of the Holy Spirit: He is the Spirit of Jehovah, of wisdom, of understanding, of counsel, of strength, of knowledge, and of the fear of the Lord (see Is. 11:2). As we will find throughout Revelation, the number *seven* is one of the several numerical values used symbolically in various prophecies. *Seven* is the number often associated with the things of God; it symbolizes the perfections of the deity. Here, as the seven-fold Spirit before the throne of God, the Holy Spirit is revealed to be a Person in the divine Godhead, perfect in holiness and power.

The amazing truth is this: It is this same Holy Spirit who comes to live within all of us who depend upon what Jesus has done to make us right with God. Since He is the *Holy* Spirit, it is plain that it is His work to *make us holy.*

The Ruling Redeemer

The third divine Person exalted by John in this doxology is the One upon whom the bulk of the prophecies **1:5** of the Revelation focus: Jesus Christ.

Jesus is praised first because He is "the faithful witness." In his Gospel, John quotes the words of Jesus to Pilate, " '... For this I have come into the world, to bear witness to the truth...' " (John 18:37). Certainly Jesus remained faithful in that witness, even to death on the Cross. Now we are called to be His witnesses in the world, and He has left us an example for us to follow in His steps (see 1 Pet. 2:21). As believers we have been left on this earth for a purpose, and part of that purpose is to "beg you on behalf of Christ, be reconciled to God" (2 Cor. 5:20). If we fail to be faithful in that duty, a major purpose in our lives may lie unfulfilled.

John next lauds Christ because He is "the first-born of the dead." He is the first to die and then rise to everlasting life. (The people who were raised from the dead before the resurrection of Jesus lived on only for a time, and then they died again. Jesus is to first come back to life in total victory over the power of death, never to taste death again.)

That Jesus is called the *"first*-born from the dead" indicates there will be others who will follow Him in the resurrection unto life. Those of us who are in vital union with Him are assured of our own resurrection on the last day (see John 6:40).

It is also significant that this idea of being raised from the dead follows after the reference to "the faithful witness." Many of those who originally heard these words literally were facing death daily. This assurance of future resurrection would have brought a specifically meaningful hope to their hearts. While thousands of Christ's people from every era have gladly given their lives for Him, many modern-day Christians cringe from bearing witness to Christ for fear of even an eyebrow being lifted against them. We need to align our priorities with those of the Scriptures, and we must assuage our fears with the promises of God.

Finally, Jesus is called "the ruler of the kings of the earth." This title of Jesus would have been especially comforting to the early church which was constantly in danger of attack from the forces of Rome. The Emperors Nero and Domitian had been particularly cruel in their dealings with the followers of Christ. But here we are reminded that even they lived and ruled under the authority of an infinitely more powerful king, our Lord Jesus Christ Himself. As Jesus told Pilate just before His crucifixion, " 'You would have no authority over Me, unless it had been given you from above' " (John 19:11).

In today's world of political unrest and uncertainty, it is imperative that we recall this title of Jesus. Whatever may befall the nations of the world, whichever political doctrine holds sway, still Jesus is in control. He is "the ruler of the kings of the earth," and those kings can do nothing which He does not allow. All authority in heaven and earth belongs to Him (see Matt. 28:18).

Downcast believer, take heart. You may have financial worries, but the One who loves you most owns the cattle on a thousand hills. You may have a grieving heart, but He who has called you by name is the gentle Comforter. Do you fear the future? He has prepared it for your glory. Are you threatened by the powers of this world? He is the ruler of the kings of the earth—and if God is for you, who can be against you (see Rom. 8:31)?

A Kingdom of Priests

According to Mosaic law, no one person was allowed to hold both of the offices of priest and king. Israel was never to have a priest who ruled nor a king who made sacrifice. This separation of church and state prevented power from becoming centralized in a single man. God alone was to be the absolute sovereign. Saul violated this principle when, as king of Israel, he personally offered sacrifice to the Lord, and in so doing performed the duties of a priest. As a result God rejected him as Israel's king and His Spirit departed from him (see 1 Sam. 13:8–14).

In the prophecy of Zechariah, however, we read an unexpected prediction. Zechariah prophesied that God would send a Man who would be *both* king and priest, One who would be "a priest on His throne" (Zech. 6:13). This One, of course, is Jesus, the great High Priest and King of the church. The Psalms also speak of the coming One who would sit on the throne of God but who would nevertheless be a priest (see 110: 1–4). This again points to the reign and intercession of Jesus on our behalf.

Because He loves us He has released us from the penalty and power of sin, and He has made us like

Himself, to be kings and priests. Imagine! We are "a **1:6**
kingdom [of] priests." Later in the Revelation we will find
that we even now reign with Christ from His heavenly **20:6**
throne, just as we will find that the church is represented **4:4**
in heaven by elders, seated on thrones, who wear king-
ly crowns of gold and the white garments of the priesthood.

What encouragement and comfort this is to us who
have by faith been eternally identified with Christ. The
most horrible tragedies we might endure in this life
pale in their insignificance when compared to that power and joy we should be experiencing in our rule with
Him (see James 1:2,3). Instead of being overcome by
our circumstances, we may rule over them as the kings
that we truly are. Instead of despairing hopelessly in
our problems, we may intercede before God on behalf of
ourselves and others—as any good priest would do. And
as we rule and minister in the name of Jesus, His reign
and ministry in our own lives will grow to its fullness.

The Return of the King

The great hope of the Christian faith is focused upon
the return of Jesus at the end of the world. On that
Last Day He will both judge the evil world by His Word
(see John 12:48) and raise up unto eternal life all those
whom the Father has drawn to Him by faith (see John
6:44).

"He is coming with the clouds, and every eye will see **1:7**
Him." Here is both the final victory for Christ's people
and the event which will strike the terror of doom into
the hearts of His enemies. But whether victor or enemy, "every eye will see Him, even those who pierced
Him." Every man and woman who has ever lived will
stand before the righteous Judge of the earth.

On that day when "time," as we experience it, ceases
and eternity is ushered in, "all the tribes of the earth

will mourn over Him." What a reversal of roles that will be! At the first coming of Christ, the world rejoiced at His death as His followers mourned. But at His second coming His people will rejoice as sin and death are put away.

He who rejoices last, rejoices best!

Everything You Need From A to Ω

As John contemplates that great day of Jesus' return, a sudden and powerful voice fills his mind; it is the voice of the Almighty. As He did earlier in this chapter, God identifies Himself as the One "who is and who **1:8** was and who is to come," but this time there is another very significant title added. He says, "I am the Alpha and the Omega." Note carefully who it is that is speaking: It is "the Lord God." What does God call Himself? He is the "Alpha and the Omega."

Alpha and omega are the first and last letters of the Greek alphabet, and this title indicates that God is all in all from beginning to end, able to be and to provide everything His people need, and deserving of all worship.

But we find what is especially noteworthy about this particular title in the very last chapter of the Revelation. There we hear Jesus saying of Himself, "I am the **22:13** Alpha and the Omega, the first and the last, the beginning and the end." Jesus Christ is Lord and God (see also John 10:30). Hence we realize this "revelation of Jesus Christ" is at the same time the revelation of God the Father Himself. As if we needed any extra encouragement to do so, John exhorts us here to heed carefully the things written in this prophecy, for they are the things of God. If you want to know God the Father, you must find Him through Jesus Christ. If you want to know Jesus Christ, the Holy Spirit speaking through the Revelation provides a perfect introduction.

John the Prophet

After this lengthy and informative doxology of praise to the triune God, John gives us a word of personal testimony concerning his circumstances as he received the visions of the Revelation.

John reveals first his attitude toward himself. He **1:9** realizes that some readers might unduly exalt him as an apostle or because he has received a direct communication from God. To counteract that potential problem John quickly identifies himself with common believers. He is our "brother," not our master, and he is a "fellow partaker" with us of the trials and joys of this world. John does not stand upon formalities or personal claims to fame.

We Christians today should take a cue here. Modern Christendom, especially in America, has developed a tendency to glamorize various religious superstars, sometimes glorifying men above the Lord. But John knew, as we should, that Jesus Christ is the only worthy object of glory. There is no other.

We also find in his self-description John's understanding of the nature of the tribulation and the kingdom of God. Rather than placing them only in the future, John acknowledges that even in the first century both trouble and the presence of the kingdom were already at hand. Tribulation in the church began with the killing of Jesus, and the kingdom was present amidst God's people when Jesus was declared with power to be the Son of God and ascended to the throne of His Father.

Since we all find ourselves, like John, in both tribulation and kingdom, as the elect of God we must also share with John the "perseverance which [is] in Jesus." It is this steadfastness to which we hold, even in the face of persecution and temptation, and which will ultimately bring us into the fullness of the kingdom.

"The one who endures to the end, he shall be saved" (Matt. 24:13).

Having thus humbly identified himself, John tells us that the visions of the Revelation came to him while he was in exile on Patmos, a postage-stamp-sized island in the Aegean Sea, off the southwest coast of modern Turkey. It is plain why John had been exiled: "because of the word of God and the testimony of Jesus."

By this time in his life, John was a very old man, probably in his eighties. Others in his circumstances might have felt it was high time to retire. But not John. For there is no such thing as an Overcomer, Rtd. He had a continuing ministry so active that it got him thrown out of his own country! It has been said that we are known by the enemies we have, as well as by the friends we keep. Do you have enough boldness for Christ to get yourself into the kind of "trouble" old John stirred up?

What the church needs today may be more such "troublemakers." It may be time once again in history to remind ourselves that we are under orders from the King of Kings to assist in His overthrow of the kingdom of this world. Let us polish up our swords, put on our armor, and get into the fight!

The Son of Man in Glory

In His incarnation Jesus took the "form of a bond-servant" (Phil. 2:7) and "the likeness of sinful flesh" (Rom. 8:3). More simply put, God the Son took on full humanity. As man, God the Son was no different from the multitudes which thronged around Him, save for His complete sinlessness. Following His resurrection and ascension, Jesus remains fully man, but now with the glory which is rightly His. His glorified humanity is described in symbolic terms by the Apostle as he encounters this One who is God and Man forever, in this first of the visions recorded in the Revelation.

John tells us that he was "in the Spirit on the Lord's   1:10
day"—Sunday. "In the Spirit" may refer to a special visionary state into which God had called John so that he
could receive the upcoming vision. The phrase may
also mean that John was "villed with the Holy Spirit"—he was yielded to the power and presence of God as
he worshipped the Lord.

In either case, John was certainly "tuned in" to the
Holy Spirit and pliable before the will of God. Although
you and I aren't prophets like John, we nevertheless
have access to the power of the same Spirit who controlled
John so long ago. We receive the Holy Spirit when, by
faith, we receive the living and resurrected Christ.

As John, then, was worshipping, he heard behind him
"a loud voice like the sound of a trumpet." It's hard to
imagine what such a voice must have sounded like, but
it would have certainly been an attention-getter. It
caught John's ear!

The voice told John to record the visions which he   1:11
would see and to circulate the resulting book among
the seven churches of Asia Minor. Who would make
such a strange request, and who could possess that
trumpet voice? John turned to find out. But he was   1:12
totally unprepared for what he saw: a dazzling Person
standing in the middle of seven golden lampstands.
Words are inadequate to describe the splendor of the
One he saw.

The first thing John tells us is that the Person before   1:13
him looked like "the Son of Man." This title was Jesus'
favorite in referring to Himself during His earthly ministry. The key to understanding what "the Son of Man"
means is found initially in the pages of the Old Testament. In the prophecy of Daniel, we are told that Daniel
had a vision during the night (see 7:13, 14). In it he saw
standing before the throne of God "One like a Son of
Man." Daniel goes on to describe the scene, telling us
that "to Him was given dominion, glory, and a kingdom, that all the peoples, nations, and men of every
language might serve Him..." (v. 14).

Does this Son of Man sound like just another member of the human race, the ordinary son of an ordinary man? Never. When Jesus Christ referred to Himself as Son of Man, He was saying, "I am the One before whom all the peoples of the earth will someday bow. My kingdom will last forever." When John turns to see the glorified Christ, he sees One who is God in His glorified humanity. This "Son of Man" is God the Son, the Ruler of all the universe!

In his description of the Son, John uses a number of word pictures which are difficult for us to grasp in our mental vision. Perhaps it is not so important that we can call up visual images of this figure or that we are able to draw a picture of Him. What is important is that we understand the significance of the language that John uses in his description. Again, John's language comes from Old Testament descriptions of God Himself, and the confirmation comes through these symbols loud and clear: Jesus, the Son of Man, is God.

The glorified Christ is described as having hair "white **1:14** like white wool" and eyes "like a flame of fire." His feet were like glowing bronze and His voice "like the sound **1:15** of many waters." Each of these figurative phrases is borrowed from an Old Testament prophet's description of the divine Being, and each points us to the true identity of Jesus Christ (see Dan. 7:9; 10:6; Ezek. 43:2).

"In His right hand He held seven stars," which we **1:16** soon find out represent the leaders of the seven churches. **1:20** This observation reminds us of Jesus' intimate concern for His people. Those shepherds of the flock appointed by Jesus are in His grasp, under His watchful care and discipline, so that they might in turn nurture Christ's church. "Out of His mouth came a sharp two-edged sword" representing the Word of God, the Bible (see Heb. 4:12). Jesus' words are God's words, and they have been inscripturated for our benefit, so that we might know the truth: Jesus' words are life and truth (see John 17:17; 6:63). "His face was like the sun shining in its strength" as it was at His Transfiguration (see Matt.

17:2), an appropriate description for the One who is the
Light of the World.

John's Fear—Christ's Comfort

Understandably, as John catches a glimpse of this   **1:17**
unearthly figure, he falls at His feet, just as if he were
dead. This is the usual response in Scripture of those
who have caught sight of the majesty of the Lord: They
realize simultaneously their own sinfulness and God's
holiness (see Acts 9:4; Is. 6:5).

But Jesus has not come to frighten John. He has
come to bring words of comfort and promise to His people. As He raises John from his knees, Christ tells him
not to fear for His life, for He is "the living One," the   **1:18**
Source and Giver of life. With His title "the first and
the last" Jesus again identifies Himself with Jehovah
(see Is. 44:6). But with His claim to be One who "was
dead" but now is "alive forevermore," He speaks of
uniquely New Testament truth. This is the resurrected
Christ, who has suffered the pangs of the Cross and the
pains of hell itself. He *was* dead, but His death was not
final. It was a prelude to resurrection and life eternal.
Because He has experienced the powers of death and
Hades and has overcome them, He has gained authority over them forever. He holds the keys to both and is
able to shut up or to set free those whom He wishes.

The comfort in all of this is the assurance that death
need not be final for me or for you. That means you! My
cousin-in-law Lorraine, a wonderful woman in the prime
of life, died of cancer last year. What can we say to
such things? Does the Revelation offer any hope to us?
Certainly. Those who belong to Christ, though we may
experience physical pain and death, will spiritually never die (see John 11:26). Jesus has overcome death and
is alive forevermore. He has undergone on our behalf
the death we deserve by our rebelliousness and attitudes of independence from Him. Jesus is therefore ab-

solutely serious when He tells us not to fear. Though He was dead, He now lives forever. The same will be true for all of us who believe in Him: Even if we die, yet shall we live (see John 11:25)!

Luminaries and Lampstands

As this first chapter in the Revelation comes to an end, Jesus presents what is in effect an introduction to His later messages to us. He tells John to write "the **1:19** things which you have seen" (the initial vision of Jesus we have just studied), "the things which are" (the conditions in the seven churches He is about to address), and "the things which shall take place after these things" (the contents of the rest of the visions, which describe the forces which are influential in the world today and which have been active since the time of John).

Finally, as if to give us a running start into the concerns of the Revelation's next two chapters, Jesus reveals the meaning of the stars and the lampstands John described earlier. "The seven stars are the angels of the seven churches, and the seven lampstands are the sev- **1:20** en churches."

The "angels [literally: messengers] of the seven churches" are symbols of the pastors or overseers of the individual congregations, while the lampstands represent the people in those churches. Jesus, in His love for His church, holds its leaders in His hand and walks among His people. He is well acquainted with our trials and our fears, for He dwells with us. He is not far off, but near. If you belong to Him, He knows you, loves you, and gives eternal life to you. You shall never perish, and no one will snatch you out of His hand (see John 10:28).

2. The Land of Ecclesia

There is a government on this earth which does not belong here. It is an outpost of an eternal kingdom, peopled by peculiar citizens who refuse to go along with the rest of the world. These people insist they follow a Monarch who teaches that the only way to live is to die, that the way to gain is to give, and that the way to become great is to become a servant. More disturbingly they say the way one gets into this kingdom is not by being "good," but rather by admitting that one is *not* good enough to get in.

The rest of the world might tolerate the existence of this kingdom, except for the fact its citizens refuse to keep such things to themselves. Its patriots have the annoying habit of successfully living their convictions, and they try to persuade the citizens of the neighboring nations to renounce that citizenship and join in as participants in this other kingdom.

Most bothersome of all is the claim of these meddlesome people that their King is rightfully the ruler, not only of their own nation, but of all the nations of the world. And there is a mystery. No one in the world today has ever seen this King. Nevertheless, His followers insist He is coming back, soon, to prove they have been right all along.

Clearly, such bizarre behavior and beliefs are "potentially dangerous" to society as a whole. So this kingdom—we'll call it the Land of Ecclesia—must be obliterated from the face of the earth.

So goes the world's understanding of the church of

Jesus Christ. And it is not difficult to see that from the unbelieving world's point of view, the church is composed of a lot of odd persons. But this "oddness" is precisely what the church is all about. In fact, the very meaning of the word *church* hints that true believers will be different from the world.

The New Testament word for "church" is *ecclesia*, a Greek word which means "the called-out ones." The church is comprised of those who have been called out of the world and into the kingdom of God, called out of a life of darkness and into His marvelous light (see 1 Pet. 2:9). Thus, if we have been called out, we no longer live as the world does.

This church/world dichotomy gives rise to the letters which Christ sends through John to the seven churches of first-century Asia Minor. Those early Christians, like us today, were far from being what they should have been. Because of this, the words Jesus speaks to them are extremely relevant to the twentieth-century Land of Ecclesia, too. Read on and see if any of these ancient churches sound like yours.

I. Ephesus: Big on Doctrine, Small on Love

The first of the seven churches Christ addresses is **2:1** the church of Ephesus. Jesus introduces Himself to this church by calling Himself "the One who holds the seven stars... the One who walks among the seven golden lampstands." We have already seen that these symbols represent the church and its appointed leaders.

In this title Christ is assuring the Ephesian church, and us today, that He is intimately aware of what is happening in our churches. Our God is not off in some corner of the universe, too busy to be bothered by the trifling troubles of a few groups of His followers. No, Jesus *knows* our ups and downs, our victories and defeats. He's aware of bills, and kids, and jobs, and housework. And He knows what to do about them.

In fact, the words "I know..." begin each of the seven 2:2
letters of Revelation 2 and 3. The first step in learning
to deal with our problems is consciously to turn them
over to the One who cares and the One who knows.

Jesus begins His address by recounting a number of
very positive things concerning the Ephesian believers.
They had worked diligently for the gospel, they had 2:3
held fast to orthodox doctrine—even in the midst of
false teaching—and they had wisely exercised church
discipline. Not bad. I would be happy to have the Lord
say those things about my church, wouldn't you?

Fixing Our Eyes

And yet there was one thing missing, one thing which
almost negated all the positive efforts this church had
made. They had left their first love. 2:4

No more tragic criticism could be brought against a
church. They had good works; they had discipline; they
had orthodoxy. But they had lost the love of Jesus. As
Paul wrote, "If I have... all knowledge; and... all
faith... but do not have love, I am nothing" (1 Cor.
13:2).

I know of churches today like this, made up of good,
hard-working people who carefully listen to the Word
of God as it is preached. These people know their doctrine. But their love for Christ, and for each other, is
lacking. They are experts on the letter of the law; they
know little of the Spirit.

Now don't get me wrong. Sound doctrine is imperative. That is clear in this letter to Ephesus, for Jesus
praises the Ephesian church for its doctrinal soundness.
But remember that by and large the Pharisees also
held to sound doctrine, and yet it is apparent that they
missed the real meaning of it all.

In His love for His church, Jesus prescribes the anti- 2:5,6
dote for this loss of love. He says that we must keep
recalling to mind the first love which we had for Christ
and the simplicity of His gospel, that we must turn
away from our cerebral coldness and return to that love

for Jesus with which He originally drew us to Himself. How is this brought about? John gives us a good starting place in another letter: "If someone says, 'I love God,' and hates his brother, he is a liar; for the one who does not love his brother whom he has seen, cannot love God whom he has not seen" (1 John 4:20). This love for the brethren is not all that love for Christ entails, but it is an essential element which seems to be sadly lacking in a significant number of Christ's churches today.

Just as the love of Christ for His church is overwhelming, so can be His discipline. When repentance and restored love are not forthcoming from His people, Jesus can and will go to the extreme of blotting out their witness: "I will remove your lampstand out of its place—unless you repent."

Overcomer or Overcome?

To those who hear and heed His words, Christ promises incredible blessings. In each of the seven letters these promises are made to "him who overcomes." The **2:7** chief overcomer is Christ Himself, who has "overcome the world" (John 16:33). As you follow Him in faith and obedience in His church, you, too, share in His victory and are an overcomer along with Him.

Every rough spot in your life is not necessarily a major life-and-death trial. I'm sure that your life, like mine, is filled more usually with a number of smaller problems, not very dramatic, but nonetheless troubling.

The secret of dealing with such daily difficulties is found in learning to be an overcomer with Christ, applying His promises to your everyday life. You may not have to escape a riotous mob as Paul did, but you may have to deal with some less than perfect teen-agers every day in your home. You may not have to defend yourself before a king like Paul did, but you might have an irksome neighbor who needs to hear what Jesus has done in your life. The promises of Christ are real in these everyday circumstances we face constantly.

Learn to depend on Him for the small things. Instead of being overcome by your circumstances, overcome them through applying God's Word. In doing so, you will be building up a storehouse of victories so that when the really tough times come, you will have a reservoir of faith upon which to draw.

Access to the Tree of Life

What is the "tree of life" which Jesus promises to those who overcome?

In the first book of the Bible, the story of Adam and Eve is told. When our first parents sinned, their fellowship with God was broken. As a result they were denied access to the tree of life which grew in the Garden of Eden. But Jesus promises that those who overcome through Christ have their relationship with the Father restored, and thus they are invited to eat of the tree—a symbol of the gift of eternal life which is bestowed upon all who follow Jesus. Its fruit was appropriately called by the ancients, "The Medicine of Immortality." This promise was valid to the people of Ephesus in the first century, and its eternal validity extends to you and me today—as we overcome with Christ.

II. Smyrna: When Death Leads to Life

Jesus introduces Himself to the church at Smyrna by this name: the One "who was dead, and has come to life." This is a significant address, for the Smyrnans were a church undergoing difficult times of tribulation. They needed to be reminded of Christ's conquering the great enemy death. For them, the possibility of being martyred for their faith was a daily reality.   **2:8**

Again, Jesus begins His words to the church by saying, "I know...." He knew of their difficult times, of their hardships, tribulation, and poverty. It is likely that many believers in Smyrna had lost their jobs because they   **2:9** refused to participate in the pagan rituals associated with their trades. (Job-related problems are nothing new!)

This church was also being attacked from the outside. The Jews of Smyrna claimed to be worshipping the true God, though they had been deceived by the Evil One into rejecting Messiah Jesus, God's Son. Theirs was no longer the synagogue of Jehovah; it had become "a synagogue of Satan," and in line with Satan's goals, they were seeking to destroy the church of Christ. Yes, the church at Smyrna was one being sorely tested and tried.

The Church Under Attack: The Tribulation

Even a cursory study of history shows that from the earliest years of the church to this present hour, the people of God have been in tribulation. The attack arises from the evil forces and influences of the world. The church of Smyrna is but one example of the multitudes of believers who throughout history have had to suffer for their faith. Christians in America are often very provincial when it comes to recognizing such trouble. We seem to say in effect, "If it's not happening to me, then it's not happening."

But speak to the dying first-century believer in Rome who had been dipped in oil and set aflame to light one of Nero's dinner parties, and tell him that he won't have to go through tribulation. Speak to our Christian brother or sister who is now shackled in some Communist "mental hospital" and tell him or her that tribulation has not yet arrived. No, tribulation for the church is upon us. And the Scriptures tell us it will increase as the end draws near.

Listen to John: "Children, it is the last hour; and just as you heard that antichrist is coming, even now many antichrists have arisen; from this we know that it is the last hour" (1 John 2:18). Hear Peter: "Beloved, do not be surprised at the fiery ordeal among you, which comes upon you for your testing, as though some strange thing were happening to you" (1 Pet. 4:12). The Smyrnan church knew these things. Perhaps our own comfortable churches will find out as well, sooner than we expect.

The Faithful Do Not Fear

Christ's words to His church are ones of encouragement: "Do not fear what you are about to suffer." Jesus **2:10** has told His people in advance that they will suffer at the hands of the Evil One, that they will be tested even to the point of death.

But there is comfort even in such apparently frightening words. If Jesus can predict the suffering which will befall His people, even down to its duration ("ten days," symbolic of a significant but limited period of time), it means that He is ultimately in control of the entire situation. His church will suffer, but not more than it can endure; His people will be tested, but they will emerge from the fires of testing purified. The very fact that you are reading these words today is testimony to God's faithfulness in delivering His promise to you!

Most of all, it must be remembered that Jesus Himself was killed at the hands of the evil world—and what was the result? Eternal honor and glory. Ultimately, the worst thing the world can do to you is to send you to heaven a little sooner than you expected to get there. No wonder Jesus says, "Do not fear...." The crown of eternal life awaits those of us who are faithful until death.

Although the death of the body awaits us, those who overcome "shall not be hurt by the second death"—hell, **2:11** the lake of fire. As someone has formulated it: "Born once, die twice; born twice, die once." We who have **20:14** been born again through trusting faith in Jesus Christ have no need to fear that second death, for there is no condemnation for those who are in Him (see Rom. 8:1).

III. Pergamum: Acceptance Without Discipline

Jesus introduces Himself to the church at Pergamum with the title, "the One who has the sharp two-edged sword." This sword represents the Word of God which   **2:12** divides between the affairs of men (see Heb. 4:12). It is also the weapon with which the church must do battle. The church at Pergamum had been lax in wielding that sword, and because of that they receive the rebuke of Christ.

Jesus knew several admirable things about the be-   **2:13** lievers in Pergamum. They lived under difficult circumstances, dwelling in a city which was the Asian center for the worship of the Roman emperor ("where Satan's throne is"). In the midst of their tribulation they had not denied the faith, even when outright persecution had broken out. This cost at least one brother, named Antipas, his life.

But still, Jesus says, "I have a few things against   **2:14** you." This church allowed teachers whose words were not in conformity to the Scriptures to instruct it. There were some who held to the "teaching of Balaam," apparently a doctrine which said that a believer could live in open compromise with the world, even to the point of participating in pagan rituals and immorality. "The teaching of the Nicolaitans" to which this church   **2:15** had fallen prey seems to be a similar aberration.

Here is a church which had withstood the attacks of the outside world only to fall captive to heresy within. There were none knowledgeable or zealous enough for the truth to discipline those who taught false doctrines. This is the opposite end of the stick from the problem with the church at Ephesus. Ephesus had good church discipline but lacked love; Pergamum, in the name of "love," accepted any teaching that came down the pike, for fear of rejecting and offending anyone. It was an

"I'm okay, you're okay," go with the flow sort of arrangement.

Doctrine and Love

Some churches today are typified by believers who say things like, "Doctrine isn't important. All we want to do is love one another." Now that may sound very pious and Christlike, but if it is, then why do we find Christ Himself rebuking a church for holding that attitude?

True love for Christ means love for His Word: " 'If you love Me, you will keep my commandments' " (John 14:15). And true love for the brethren means obeying that Word in our lives so that we might be pleasing to the Lord.

Discipline, according to the Pastoral Epistles of 1 and 2 Timothy and Titus, is a mark of the true church of Christ. When we hear any teaching we must be like the Bereans of Paul's acquaintance who, when they heard him speak, examined the Scriptures to see if what he said was true (see Acts 17:11). If we find that a teaching is false when compared with the truth of Scripture, we must reject it. It must be exorcised from the life of the church. This is true love for Christ and for His children. We cannot let fear of offending our friends cause us to offend God. The church of Pergamum needed to learn that truth. We need it as well today.

Warning and Promise

The church is explicitly told what to do to overcome   2:16
this particular sin: *repent*. Repentance is turning away from sin. In this instance, it involved turning away from false teaching by removing the bogus teachers from the church. If that was not done, Jesus warned, He *personally* would apply the needed discipline by making war against the false teachers. This warning should caution anyone who would presume to teach the Word of God to others. He or she had better do the homework, knowing that a teacher incurs a stricter judgment (see James 3:1). We should not be "supportive" or "affirming"

of just anyone, merely because he claims to be a "Bible teacher." We must compare all teaching with the Word of God.

But again there is a gracious promise from Jesus which accompanies His warning. We who overcome will receive the "hidden manna," Jesus Himself, "the living **2:17** bread that came down out of heaven" (John 6:51). We will also receive a "white stone," the ancient symbol of innocence in a court of law. For Christ's sake, God has declared us "not guilty." Because one has partaken of the Bread of Life, he is declared righteous by the Father and thus shares in the righteousness of Christ. this promise is to all who are faithful and obedient until the end, and it is to this day graciously offered to you and me.

IV. Thyatira: Compromise With the World

In significant ways the church at Thyatira was like the one in Pergamum. Both churches are commended: They had persevered in the face of outside attack and had not denied the faith. They believed in Christ crucified and risen. Both Pergamum and Thyatira also have a negative report to deal with: There was a toleration of false teaching in both churches, a situation which threatened to bring the discipline of the Lord upon them.

But one characteristic is revealed about Thyatira which was apparently not the case with Pergamum. The Thyatiran church seems to have been *divided* doctrinally over the false teaching issue. This point makes the letter to this church of great relevance to our twentieth-century church scene.

As the letter begins, Jesus calls Himself "The Son of **2:18** God, who has eyes like a flame of fire and His feet are like burnished bronze." This title is a reference to the description of the glorified Christ that was given us by John in Revelation 1. This awesome description of Jesus, along with the use of His name, the Son of God, is calculated to get the serious attention of the Thyatirans—and ours as well. This is no self-appointed teacher rendering his opinion on such-and-such a matter; this is God Himself laying down the law! We had best listen and obey.

Jesus commends the church for its strengths: In many 2:19 ways it had grown and matured. In fact, its "deeds of late are greater than at first." Compare this with the situation in Ephesus, where the believers were exhorted to return to their former deeds, having fallen away from their loving zeal for the Lord. In Thyatira there were problems, but the Lord is not willing to give up on these people.

Taking the Easy Way Out

A good number in the church in Thyatira had fallen under the spell of someone who is called "the woman 2:20 Jezebel." This "Jezebel" may have been an actual person, or possibly this was a name used to refer to false teaching among the people of God, such as Jezebel of the Old Testament promoted (see 1 Kin. 16:31,32).

In any case, the teaching of Jezebel was leading astray the sheep of Christ's flock in Thyatira. The nature of this false teaching apparently had to do with the compromise of Christian values and behavior with those of the unbelieving world. We are told that acts of immorality and the eating of things sacrificed to idols were special signs of this heresy. What are we to make of this?

In first century Thyatira, as in many ancient cities, trade guilds had developed which claimed the allegiance of all local craftsmen of a certain skill. To hold a job, a man had to be a member of the appropriate guild. The Christian's problems arose with the fact that each guild had its patron god or goddess, and the members of the guild were required to worship their special deity and to participate in immoral feasts in honor of their god.

Both of these pagan practices were taboo for the follower of Christ—which meant, no doubt, that many church
families had fathers and husbands who were currently
unemployed.

At this point the teaching of Jezebel enters the scene.
Apparently some factions in the church began to teach
it was all right to take part in such worldly activity as
long as one did not actually *deny* Jesus with his words.
In other words, said Jezebel, you can be *in* the world
and *of* it, too—as long as you go through the formal
motions of Christianity.

What About Us?

Participation in pagan rituals of immorality might
seem to be quite far from the dangers to the contemporary
American believer. But I wonder. It may well be that Jezebel yet lives!

A great many believers today are involved in a game
of spiritual brinksmanship: How close can I come to
being like the world without really falling into it? Instead of fleeing from the fire of sin, we see how close we
can get without being singed. The smooth words of Jezebel fall upon too many eager ears today.

Loving but Stern Discipline

The church at Thyatira had already been warned
about their problem, but they had been slow in dealing   **2:21**
with it. Too slow. Now Jesus Himself comes to apply the
needed discipline. It was plain that those taking the
easy road of compromise had no intention of returning
to the narrow way, so Christ announces the "get tough"
measures which He is about to implement.

When repentance for sin is not forthcoming from a   **2:22,**
professing believer, Christ is willing to go to the ex-   **23**
treme of bringing about the sickness, even the death, of
the unrepentant brother or sister. This apparently is
Paul's meaning when he speaks of those who were mak-

ing a mockery of Holy Communion: "For this reason many among you are weak and sick, and a number sleep" (1 Cor. 11:30).

Our mental images of "gentle Jesus, meek and mild" need revision. While "God is love" (1 John 4:8), He is also "a consuming fire" (Heb. 12:29), tender in His care, but stern in His judgments. As Peter reminds us, "It is time for judgment to begin with the household of God" (1 Pet. 4:17). God is not merely concerned with making you *happy.* He wants to make you *holy!* He disciplines us that we might share in His holiness (see Heb. 12:10).

The Faithful Few

Despite this apostasy among the Thyatirans, there   **2:24** remained some in that church who had not soiled their garments with sin. Jesus encourages them by refusing to burden them with any prohibitions. He merely ex-   **2:25** horts them to hold fast to that which they had already received: the good news of the gospel.

And so it is with you and me. Victory in Christ is not some mystical new truth. It is not asceticism and legalistic abstention from that which is not forbidden. It is rather a consistent walk with Jesus Christ. It is living out what the Scriptures teach.

It often appears that we Christians are at the mercy   **2:26,27** of the world-system which surrounds us. But in the end it will be revealed that true authority resides in Jesus and in those who belong to Him. Since Jesus has received "all authority . . . in heaven and on earth" (Matt. 28:18), He is free to dispense a measure of that authority to us who have overcome through Him.

With that authority we also receive "the morning   **2:28** star," an ancient symbol of royalty. Just as He disciplines us that we might share in His holiness, so He redeems us that we might share in His reign. The Son of God has become the Son of Man, that the children of mankind might become the children of God.

V. Sardis: Death in the Pew

Jesus introduces Himself to the church at Sardis by saying that He is the One "who has the seven Spirits of **3:1** God." This title of Jesus is very significant in light of the problems faced by this church. The flame of the Spirit of Life had flickered in Sardis and was close to being extinguished.

It is noteworthy that in contrast to the other churches we have studied, Sardis is not said to be under any kind of attack, either from without or from within. This is a respectable, middle-of-the-road, peaceful church. But its peace is like unto that of a cemetery. Bluntly, Jesus has little good to say about these Christians. Instead He chides them: "You have a name that you are alive, but you are dead."

Here is a group of professing believers merely going through the motions of religion. They were no doubt regular in their attendance at worship; they gave to the needs of the poor; they were polite to their neighbors. (This is probably why they were not being persecuted. Satan loves to have us all vaccinated with a little *religion*, to keep us from catching the *real* thing.)

In other words, the congregation at Sardis appears to be a fine church. But God does not look on the outward appearance—and Jesus warns Sardis, "I have not found **3:2** your deeds completed in the sight of My God." According to man's perspective, everything was fine. But when God looked into the hearts of these people, He saw that they were nearly dead. These were ones of whom Paul spoke, that they are "holding to a form of godliness, although they have denied its power" (2 Tim. 3:5).

Does this describe any church members of your acquaintance? What about you? Are you as zealous in proclaiming Christ as you are in sticking up for your pet doctrine? Do you guard wholeheartedly the outward forms of your religion, but fail to walk daily in the Spirit?

The church at Sardis was clothed with all the trappings of religiosity, but some of the folks there were more interested in being "good church members" than in becoming good Christians.

The subtlety of Satan is amazing—he would be glad for us to be upstanding Presbyterians or Baptists or Methodists, so long as we don't become real Christians!

Wanted: Not Dead, but Alive

Even though the church at Sardis was in dire straits, Jesus again offers hope. Those first-century church members needed to "get back to basics." They needed to **3:3** remember the gospel which they had originally heard and lay hold of it again as if it were their only hope. (It *was!*) It was time to turn away from their spiritual apathy, to stop merely "playing church." The One who has the seven Spirits of God can give again that life-bearing Spirit to those who seek it with all their hearts. If they do not, the warning is clear: Christ will come not in blessing, but in judgment.

A few in Sardis, however, even in that slumbering church, were yet awake and well. The promise to them **3:4–6** (and us) culminates with walking in the presence of Jesus. Because we have been seeking Him all along, He permits Himself to be found. He will clothe us in the pure white garments of His righteousness, and our names will be inscribed for eternity in the Book of Life— for we will never die. And Jesus Himself, in the presence of the angels of heaven and the Father Almighty, will welcome us, "Well done, good and faithful slave" (Matt. 25:21).

VI. Philadelphia: The Strength of Weakness

From the world's perspective, the church of Philadelphia was probably the least significant of the seven churches of the Revelation. Philadelphia was a small city, not sharing the commercial or political importance of the others. But in contrast to the viewpoint of the world, Jesus reserves His greatest tribute for this church.

It is known that the believers at Philadelphia were zealous for missionary activity, even in the first century. Therefore it is fitting that here Jesus calls Himself the One "who has the key of David, who opens and no **3:7** one will shut, and who shuts and no one opens." God had used this small body of believers to open the door for the gospel into the province of Asia Minor. "The key of David" (see also Is. 22:22) refers to the key to the temple in Jerusalem, the place of God's presence among His people. Now Jesus holds that key. He is the only One who can bring us into the presence of the Lord God through the *new* temple, His church.

Because of the faithfulness of these Philadelphian **3:8** Christians, Christ prospered them. Though they had "little power" from the human point of view, they had persevered in their obedience and faith in Jesus. The blessing of God was upon them.

Contrast this church with Sardis. To the outward appearance, Sardis seemed to have it made, while Philadelphia appeared ineffectual. Sardis was not under attack, but Philadelphia had been persecuted by the Jews. Sardis had "a name;" Philadelphia did not. Yet, to Sardis Jesus said, "You are dead," and to Philadelphia He said, "I have loved you." **3:9**

How different our perceptions are from the Lord's. When we sense that our churches are beginning to struggle, we start new programs or have a "visitors' Sunday" or fire the pastor. But Jesus says that He will prosper us when we keep His Word and do not deny His name. Could it be that we in our day have failed to do that for which the Philadelphians were praised?

As a demonstration of His faithfulness, Jesus promised the Philadelphians that those Jews according to the flesh who had persecuted their church would someday acknowledge that the living God was with them, in His church. This assurance no doubt encouraged this church to continue in their faithful witness, knowing that the Lord was mindful of them, and that in the end He would exalt them.

In addition, these Christians had "kept the word of My perseverance." Instead of quitting, they kept going through the times of God's warning judgments against "those who dwell upon the earth." **3:10**

At the return of Christ, the victor's crown belongs to all of us who have followed Him to the end. We will become "pillars" in the very temple of God, enjoying His company forever, and we will be branded with the names of God, our new "hometown" (Jersusalem), and Jesus Himself. There will be no question as to where we dwell, nor to whom we belong. **3:11 3:12**

The crucial point is this: It is only our trusting and obedient belief in Jesus today which offers us the assurance of heaven for eternity. Jesus taught this truth to His loved ones in ancient Philadelphia; He would have us learn it as well.

VII. Laodicea: No Fence Sitters Allowed

The last of the seven churches to be addressed is the church of Laodicea. This city was prominent and vastly wealthy, the home of the rich. It was famous for its production of an expensive black wool for the garment industry, and it was the location of a well-known medical school, noted for its treatment of eye diseases. Laodicea was perhaps the most opulent Asian city of its day.

As Jesus opens His address to the church at Laodicea, He refers to Himself as "the faithful and true Witness." This is indeed spoken in irony, for the Laodicean church had been anything but faithful and true to their Lord. As a matter of fact, the major complaint that Jesus has against this church is that it has really been neither faithful nor unfaithful, neither true nor false. It has been neutral. **3:14 3:15**

Jesus tells them, "I would that you were cold or hot.

So because you are lukewarm... I will spit you out of   **3:16**
My mouth." This is not pleasant language, and it is not
meant to be.

How About a Nice, Tepid Drink?

The Laodiceans knew the meaning of lukewarmness.
Nearby was a river which flowed from the mountains
and offered refreshingly cold water. On the other side of
town were hot springs which relaxed the weary body.
But flowing out of Laodicea itself was a lukewarm stream,
good for no purpose. A drink of cold water on a hot day
can keep us going, and a cup of hot tea in the winter
keeps us from freezing. But who wants a drink of room-
temperature water?

It is to this type of unpalatable lukewarmness that
Jesus compares the Laodicean church. If they had been
"hot," on fire for the Lord, they certainly could have
been useful for the kingdom of Christ. Even if they had
been "cold" toward the Word of God, totally rejecting it,
at least there would have been the chance that they
might have seen the error of their ways and been converted. But because they were not really hot, they saw
no need to go out of their way to serve Christ, and
because they were not really cold they felt no need for
conversion. No wonder Jesus wanted to spit (literally,
"vomit") them out of His mouth!

Lukewarm: The Fashionable Temperature

The people of Laodicea, like many Americans today,
lived in the midst of a cultured and conservative society. Moderation was the name of the game, and religion
was definitely one of those things about which one was
to be moderate. You know—"It's not nice to be an athe-
ist, but there is no need to be a religious fanatic, either." Sound familiar? The Laodicean church didn't need
Jesus; they had religion, no more and no less than they
wanted.

Things really haven't changed all that much since the days of Laodicea's prime, have they? Hundreds of churches pay their pastors large sums of money to protect them from a real encounter with the living God. It's just so much easier and more fashionable. Put in your hour per week, drop your dues in the plate, and don't be bothered until another seven days have passed.

Poor, Naked, and Blind

How does someone who has been lukewarm for so long ever get hot? Jesus told the Laodiceans what to do.

First, they had to get rid of their attitude of self-sufficiency. "I am rich . . . and have need of nothing" was 3:17 their creed. Jesus points to the contrary: They were "poor" (in the city of opulence) and "blind" (with a famous eye clinic in their midst) and "naked" (in the home of a great clothing industry). Jesus saw through the external trappings to the essence of the problem.

The Laodiceans were called upon to exchange what they had been relying upon for that which was truly 3:18 reliable. The "gold" which Jesus gives makes one truly rich. The "white garments" with which He clothes us cover our spiritual nakedness, wrapping us in His righteousness. And the "eyesalve" which He uses to anoint our eyes brings us to the true light.

Next, they had to repent. Notice that it is the *love* of Jesus which causes Him to rebuke harshly the Laodi- 3:19 cean church. Those who turn from their fence-sitting independence, who open the doors of their lives that He might "come in . . . and . . . dine" with them, are the ones 3:20 who will share His throne and His glory! The final 3:21 message is: It's not too late. Open your heart to Christ. Even if you've been on the fence for years, with His help you can still see things changed. If you will open that door which has been closed (or perhaps barely cracked open) for so long, He will come in and make all things new — including you.

Church History Repeats Itself

It should be plain by now that the problems faced by the Christians of Asia Minor in the first century are the same ones believers wrestle with today. Because the struggles are so similar, the Lord's answers to us are like the ones He gave to His people so long ago.

Some contemporary observers bemoan the decrepit condition of the modern church; others say that we are on the verge of an unprecedented revival. I'm no prophet. I don't claim to know what is about to happen. But I do know that Jesus is still the Lord, and that He is still lovingly concerned for His church. If you as His child will take seriously both His encouragements and His warnings, He will fulfill His promises to you as an individual, and to your congregation.

Be an overcomer with Him. In this world, and in the world to come.

3. Growing Strong through Weakness

"Look! Up in the sky! It's a bird...it's a plane..." and the next line we all know: "No, it's Superman!"

Superman is doubtless the "super-est" of American superheroes. Faster than a speeding bullet, and able to leap tall buildings in a single bound and bend steel in his bare hands. Who can compare with this strange visitor from the planet Krypton?

And it is not only Superman's physical prowess which commands admiration. He has devoted himself to fighting for truth, justice, and the American way. Surely this man could rule the world!

The Clark Kent Syndrome

But it is at this point that an unexpected fact concerning Superman comes into play: *No one in Metropolis knows who he is.* In fact, his identity is kept secret from all the world (except, of course, those of us who are in the know!).

Who would guess that he is Clark Kent, that shy, bumbling, mild-mannered reporter for the *Daily Planet.* Apparently no one. Why not? Because no one expects that such strength and nobility of purpose could be found in one so humble and unassuming as Mr. Kent. Even his closest friends do not perceive who he really is. It is only when he sheds his gray business-as-usual suit and dons his otherworldly garb that the Man of Steel sets hearts fluttering and imaginations soaring.

We who study the Revelation, we who would know

Jesus Christ, can learn a lesson from Clark Kent and his alter-ego. *True strength is often expressed in seeming weakness.* Might does not always make right; rather, it is right which makes might. This is the lesson of the Clark Kent Syndrome, and it is also the lesson for us in the fourth and fifth chapters of the Revelation.

The Open Door of Heaven

In the previous chapter, we heard the words of the Lord Jesus to His churches in first-century Asia Minor. John faithfully recorded all that Jesus commissioned him to say from his island of exile.

But now the scene changes dramatically. Whereas **4:1** John had been speaking with Christ on Patmos, now he mysteriously is transported into the very throne room of heaven itself. The voice of Christ has summoned him. And as John peers upward he sees in his vision a doorway. It is through this door that John is welcomed into the presence of the Almighty and His angels! (Let me pause here just long enough to say that if you are in Christ, you will someday pass through this "door" as well.)

As John ascends to the heavenly temple, Jesus tells him his purpose in being called. He is to learn "what must take place after these things," after the various problems in those Asian churches have been resolved. It is within this context that John receives the visions which comprise the remainder of the book of Revelation. In a sense, Revelation 4 and 5 serve as an introduction to the rest of the book. These chapters introduce us to the Father on the throne and to the victorious co-reigning Lamb. They also present us with the astounding truth that you and I can also sit on thrones as overcomers with the Lamb. We can learn now, in this life, to reign over the trials of this world, to overcome every one of them through Christ.

Such a beautiful and encouraging promise is not merely

some future pie in the sky when you die. It was given instead to the Christians of the world in which John lived, and to you and me today. More than just a preview of coming attractions, Revelation is a book about today. Its truth has been meaningful to every generation of believers since John.

The All-Powerful God

Immediately upon hearing the command of Jesus to "come up" into the heavens, John finds himself in a place which his senses can scarcely comprehend. John is dazzled by the splendor surrounding him. But when his eyes finally focus, the first thing he sees is "One sitting on the throne." **4:2**

Have you ever had the feeling that your life, your kids, your job, your world, has gotten out of control? Where is God when things really get tough?

In Revelation 2 and 3 we learned of many problems experienced in the early church—problems we face today as well. We saw that the church was (and is) under attack from within and without, to the point that some believers had been called upon to give their lives for the name of Christ. The church (and the world around it) seemed to be falling apart. But what does John see? He sees a throne—and *it is not empty*. Someone is sitting upon it, and that Someone is God Almighty.

When my three friends died in their fall from the flaming gondola of that hot air balloon, they leaped into the arms of Jesus. When my mother-in-law succumbed to cancer, she fell asleep to wake up in the presence of her Lord and those who had gone on before her. Tragedy is turned into triumph when we remember who God is and what He can do. He has not lost hold. As it was with John in this vision, so it is with us: The Lord is in control.

As his eyes further take in his supernatural surroundings, John describes for us the appearance of this One **4:3** on the throne. The symbols used portray the nature of the Father. This use of imagery helps visualize that which we are told. It is impossible to put into mere words. The value of a symbol is its ability to carry great meaning which goes beyond the symbol itself. That is how the Bible sets forth these figures.

John first describes God in terms of two types of stone, the jasper and the sardius. Later in the Revelation, the jasper is described as being "crystal clear," while the sardius is blood red. These stones tell us that God is pure and holy (the crystal-clear jasper) and that He is a just God who brings judgment upon those who oppose Him (the blood-red sardius). Here is a God to be reckoned with, awesome in His righteousness and power.

But He is also a God of grace and mercy. The "rainbow around the throne" is a reminder of the promise of God to Noah, sealed by the rainbow, that He would not again destroy the world by flood (see Gen. 9:12–17). It calls to mind also His promise to never destroy those who believe in His Son, for we shall "not perish, but have eternal life" (John 3:16).

Twenty-Four Elders: The Church Enrolled in Heaven

All around the throne of God, John sees twenty-four **4:4** thrones, occupied by "twenty-four elders." We find that these elders represent the congregation of God in both the Old and the New Testaments. How do we know? Here in Revelation is introduced the number *twelve*, which represents the people of God. Recall there were *twelve* tribes in the Old Testament and *twelve* apostles in the New, both forming the foundations for God's people in their times.

In this particular vision, we know that these twenty-four elders represent God's People:

(1) Because there are elders (rulers) in both the Old and New Testament congregations.

(2) Because there are twenty-four of them—twelve for Old Testament Israel plus twelve for the New Testament church.

In addition, it is evident these elders are ministering to the Lord, for they wear the "white garments" of holy priesthood and the "golden crowns" of kingship. We who belong to Christ enjoy such favored position: As members of His church we sit in His presence, sharing in His glory and in His reign. This is why Peter calls us a "royal priesthood" (see 1 Pet. 2:9), and John says we are "a *kingdom* of priests." **1:6**

We are quickly reminded of His unique majesty and glory. "From the throne proceed flashes of lightning and sounds and peals of thunder." He is a God to be worshipped, and to be feared. For in front of the throne, as if to separate the Holy God from His fallen creation, is "a sea of glass like crystal." God has allowed Himself to be approached by sinful men through His covenant with us, but we must never forget that we are the creatures and He is the Creator. **4:5** **4:6**

We should never use God's mercy and forgiveness as a license for sin. I recently counseled a man who had committed the sin of adultery. Instead of being truly repentant, he was rather unconcerned about his sin. "God will forgive me," he said, "so it doesn't matter what I do." This is certainly a misunderstanding of the grace and mercy of God.

The gap which separates our finite natures from God's eternal nature is greater than the one which exists between the highest seraph and the lowliest amoeba; it is an infinite gap. Only because of the sacrifice of Jesus Christ on our behalf are we able to be received into the Father's presence. Even then we must not become too familiar with Him, for He is the Lord God Almighty. Though we may enter boldly into His presence because of what Christ has done (see Heb. 4:16), we must do so with great awe and respect. If we are to be wise with eternal wisdom, we must remember "the fear of the Lord is the beginning of wisdom" (Prov. 9:10).

The Four Living Creatures: All Creation Before Its God

Now, John looks closer to see even nearer the throne "four living creatures." These creatures are angelic beings, very similar in their appearance to certain angels spoken of in the prophecy of Ezekiel (see 1:5–10; 10:12–14). Of primary concern is what the presence of these creatures before God means to us.

We are told that these four living creatures resemble four earthly creatures: the lion, the calf (or ox), man, and the eagle. Of what significance could these figures be? There is an ancient rabbinic proverb which says, "The strongest of creatures is the lion, the most useful of creatures is the ox, the swiftest of creatures is the eagle, and the most intelligent of creatures is man." This vision carries the same idea. These beings are representative of various aspects of creation. In fact, these four creatures stand for *all* of creation. This is clear because the number four is frequently symbolic of the whole of the world (the four corners of the earth, the four winds, etc.).

What is it these four creatures are doing in the presence of God? Like the six-winged seraphs of Isaiah's vision (see Is. 6:1–3), they are exalting God, crying out continually, "Holy, holy, holy, is the Lord God, the Almighty...." **4:8**

Unfortunately, in this world we see little of such praise for God. Most of us have sought to lift up ourselves instead of our Creator and Lord. In this heavenly scene, however, things are as they should be: The creation symbolized here gives "glory and honor and thanks to **4:9** Him who sits on the throne, to Him who lives forever

and ever." Unlike sinful and rebellious men, the beings
in the throne room of God know better than to attempt
to exalt themselves. Their focus is, as ours must be,
praise and glory to the One who reigns forever and
ever.

The Song of the Elders: Stanza One

Imagine the sensory overload John must have been
experiencing during this vision. First, as he was caught
up into heaven, his eyes could scarcely take in the splendor around him. Then as the beauty engulfing him
began to register visually, his ears picked up the constant "holy, holy, holy" of the four living creatures. Now,
as John's attention is drawn back to the twenty-four
elders who were seated on their thrones, he finds that   4:10
they have fallen on their faces before God and that
they, too, have begun singing a song of praise.

Before we look at the lyrics of their song, we should
note what these elders do as they fall in worship. We
are told that they "cast their crowns before the throne."
What should we learn from this?

Earlier in this vision we saw the twenty-four elders   4:4
wearing the crowns of gold, indicating that they, as
representatives of the people of God, reign with their
Savior. It is plain to them, as it should be to us, that the
privileges enjoyed by us in the church are not earned
by our own doing. They are, like all expressions of the
grace of God, free gifts from Him. The elders cast their
crowns before the Lord, returning to Him what is already
His, to indicate they fully understand this truth. Any
glory which you and I enjoy must be acknowledged as
coming from the Father, the source of every good and
perfect gift (see James 1:17).

We are designed to be mirrors, reflecting the bright-
ness of God's light. No one looks at a mirror to see the
glass itself, but rather to see the image it reflects. As
mirrors of God, we must not seek to draw attention to

ourselves, but to Him who has enlightened us. We must cast our "crowns," those things in which we might personally glory, before the Lord God, acknowledging Him as our Creator. Thus, we "fall down before Him"— make ourselves low that He may be lifted up. I pray that our understanding of this vision will aid us in comprehending the awesome glory of our triune God.

Finally, we hear through John the words to the song **4:11** of the elders. It is a doxology, a song of praise. It ascribes to God "glory and honor and power." These attributes of God were important for the ancient church to understand. These churches had very little power, but they knew that their God was omnipotent. I wonder if many of our churches today, with the prestige and clout that they carry, haven't forgotten how to rely on the power of the Father. God save us from becoming religious experts, so proficient in our religiosity that we think we no longer need the strength of the Lord. This happened to the Pharisees of old, and we are not immune from the disease of self-confidence.

In the elders' glorification, God is "worthy" to receive praise because He is the Creator and Sustainer of all things. He is the Source of all life, both temporal and eternal, both physical and spiritual. Whatever is, God declared it to be so. Thus, we have here an affirmation that it is not evil which rules the world, but supreme righteousness. Despite temporal appearances to the contrary, God, the One who created and continues to uphold all things, is on His throne. He is in control.

The Search: Who Is Worthy?

After hearing the elders' song John returns his at- **5:1** tention to the throne. He notices the One seated upon the throne has an unopened book in His hand, one sealed up with seven seals. The opening of the seven seals of this book is the focus of the next vision. The central concern of the moment is to find someone able to break the seals and reveal the contents of the book.

An angel standing in the presence of God calls out for a search to be made of the universe to find one worthy to open the book. Surely whoever is able to break the seal will be mighty, for even the strong angel commanding the search is not able to open the volume. **5:2**

Inquiry is made throughout creation—"in heaven, or on the earth, or under the earth"—but still no one is found powerful enough to accomplish the task. It appears that none is worthy to break the seals and reveal the book's contents. **5:3**

Understandably, John is upset. He begins to weep. Imagine: He is called into heaven to receive a great revelation from God. He is about to learn the future history of the world and of the church, contained in this sealed book. But no one is able to look into it to tell him about what it contains. No wonder he is disappointed! **5:4**

As the tears fill John's eyes one of the elders tells him to stop crying. Someone has arrived in the throne room who has the authority to open the book. He "has overcome" and is therefore worthy to break the seals and reveal the contents of the pages within. Who could this mighty one be? Before John can ask, the elder tells him: It is "the Lion that is from the tribe of Judah, the Root of David." **5:5**

Now John begins to wipe away the tears from his eyes. He can scarcely wait to see this awesomely powerful and ferocious Lion who is able to succeed where the rest of the universe fails. As John's eyes are opened, they search out the whereabouts of this mighty Lion. But where is He? There is no Lion to be seen. **5:6**

What John does see is a Lamb, standing in the middle of the throne. A *Lamb?* And not only a Lamb, but one which has been slain. How could this Lamb have strength enough to break the mysterious seals and open the enigmatic book? A Lion might be so strong, but a Lamb—never.

The Secret of Strength

It is this vision of the slain Lamb which contains the theme of the entire Book of Revelation. That theme is this: The Lamb, apparently weak and defeated, turns out to be a Lion. He opens and controls the book of destiny, and He slays the wicked dragon which has corrupted the earth. Therefore because we are on the side of the Lamb, though we may seem weak and defeated from the human perspective, we will nevertheless overcome with the Lamb, reign with Him, and ultimately with Him defeat the dragon, Satan. Through Jesus we are overcomers. This is a message of comfort, hope, and victory. True strength often lies in seeming weakness.

This truth was of supreme importance to the first-century church. Here was a church in the midst of a hostile world, being attacked from all sides. The mighty of the Roman Empire were aligned against it, and the powerful Jews sought its destruction. What hope was there for this young and weak body of Christ's people?

From the human viewpoint, there was little. But that is precisely the point: God wants us to learn to look on things not from the human perspective, but according to the heavenly viewpoint. If what looks like a slain lamb is really the mightiest being in the universe, then perhaps there is a chance for the church—maybe there is hope for you and me! When all appears hopeless, there is still hope. The Lamb is really the Lion.

In fact, it is because the Lamb has been slain that He is vested with such power. Though slain, He is standing. This paradox reminds us that "all authority in heaven and on earth" has been given to Him (Matt 28:18). If resurrection is to take place, death must precede it. If might is to be strong, it must be expressed through weakness. This is true in the life and death of Jesus, and it must be true in your life and mine as well.

The teaching is not new with Revelation. Jesus had already explained this paradoxical principle to His disciples when He told them that if they wished to become great, they must become servants. If they desired to be first, they must make themselves last (see Mark 10:43, 44). Overcoming comes through servanthood; true strength comes through willing weakness.

The reason this principle is so important, not only to the early church, but to us today as well, is this: *Not everyone can be strong in the world's terms, but anyone can be weak.* If power belonged only to the strong, then the weak of the world would have no hope. But Revelation teaches us that true spiritual strength comes through the admission of weakness, for, as Paul says, "When I am weak, then I am strong" (2 Cor. 12:10). Such strength comes only from the Lord Jesus, not from the world. Since anyone can be weak, then in receiving that strength one must humble himself, admitting his weakness before God, and God's strength will be made available to him. "God is opposed to the proud, but gives grace to the humble" (James 4:6).

This is why a slain Lamb can defeat a hideous dragon, and it is why we must, like Paul, boast in our weaknesses rather than in our supposed strengths. The Lord Himself has said, ' "My grace is sufficient for you, for power is perfected in weakness' " (2 Cor. 12:9). This spiritual principle is afforded its greatest illustration in the life and death of Jesus, the Lamb of God, who was slain, but now has risen to be the Sovereign of the universe. If you and I are to share in His resurrection, we must first share in His humility and death to sin. This is the secret of spiritual strength.

The Lamb's Horns and Eyes

By now we should have noticed a couple of rather anomalous things about the Lamb in John's vision of the heavenly throne room. First, He is called a Lion, when to all appearance He is not. Second, although He has been slain, He is still standing. Now we discover two more strange things about Him: He has "seven horns and seven eyes."

In the first vision of this book we found that the number *seven* has a significant meaning in Revelation. It is often considered to be "the number of God" because it is a number associated with the idea of perfection. If a thing is said to be sevenfold, it is divinely perfect and complete. For example, most of the visions of the Revelation are made up of seven parts each, signifying this unfolding of the perfect plan of God for the age in which we live.

Here, in the current vision, we find that the Lamb possesses seven horns and seven eyes. What do these "sevens" signify? In the ancient world the "horn" was considered to be a symbol of power, and the "eye" was a symbol of knowledge. When we are told that the Lamb has seven horns, then we are to understand that He is perfect in His power. He is possessor of the divine omnipotence. In the same way, as we learn that the Lamb has seven eyes, we are to perceive that He has perfect knowledge. He has the omniscience of God. Therefore, both of these symbols point to the truth that Jesus Christ, the Lamb, is God. As such, He deserves the same worship the Father does. The rest of the vision develops this theme more fully.

The Song of the Elders: Stanza Two

As John watches, the omnipotent, omniscient Lamb **5:7** approaches the throne of the Father and takes the sealed book from His hand. This in and of itself is significant. The fact that the Lamb lays hold of the book without being prevented by the One on the throne indicates that He is acknowledged by the Father to be the "worthy" one. The unity of purpose shared by the Lamb and the Father on the throne is evident. Both desire for the book to be opened and recognize that the Lamb is the One to do it. We see that the will of the Father and the

Eternal Son is undivided, just as Jesus said: "I and the Father are one" (John 10:30).

The taking of the sealed book by the Lamb is imme- **5:8** diately interpreted in this same way by the watching throng of elders and angels. As He takes the book, they realize that this Lamb is indeed the "Overcomer." They burst into a second doxology of praise, similar to the first, but now directed to the Lamb instead of to the One on the throne.

This song is specifically said to be a new one. Whereas the first song has been heard in heaven since the beginning of Creation, this second one is sung now for the first time. Why is that? In terms of the vision, Jesus Christ, the slain Lamb, has just entered heaven following His death, resurrection, and ascension. Thus, since He has newly acomplished salvation for His people by the sacrifice of Himself, it is appropriate for the heavenly hosts to laud His recently won victory over death and the Evil One with a new song.

Notice the first words of this stanza. They are the **5:9** same as those of the first song: "Worthy art Thou...." The first song was addressed to God the Creator, but the second is sung to God the *Redeemer*. Whatever His activity, the God who has made us and redeemed us is worthy of all praise and honor. Every man knows God as the Creator (see Rom. 1:18–20), but only those who have been found by Jesus know Him as Savior. Jesus is to be worshipped as God, for He is both Creator and Redeemer (see Col. 1:13–16).

This new song of the elders tells us the reason the Lamb is considered worthy to take and open the book. It is no small thing that He is able to do this, for He has bought the privilege at a dear price. He "wast slain, and didst purchase for God with (His) blood men from every tribe and tongue and people and nation" (see also Gal. 3:13). It was Christ's death which led to life for so many, and it was His willing humiliation which led to His eternal exaltation.

He came to purchase men and women and children

from every period of history and from every people of
the earth. This truth must have sounded strange to
some first-century hearers who had understood that it
was *physical* Israel which would receive the promises of
God. But we learn here that God is in the process of
building a new nation, a *spiritual* Israel. The Lamb
"hast made them to be a kindgom and priests to our God;   5:10
and they will reign upon the earth."

This new Israel is not like the old one, which was
made up of the descendants of Abraham according to
the flesh. The new Israel is peopled instead by those of us
who are the spiritual descendants of "Abraham, the
believer," regardless of physical lineage (Gal. 3:9,29).
These followers of the Lamb reign upon the earth now—
though that reign is hidden from the world—and we
will rule the new earth for all eternity, following the   21:1,
destruction of this present world.   22:5

What a future awaits us who overcome through the
victory of the Lamb! Though we often appear to be
weak as lambs in the world's eyes, the day is approaching
when we will be revealed as the sons and daughters of
God, ruling the earth in His stead (see 1 John 3:2). This
is the promise of Christ to all of us who are faithful
until death. Why, then, do you worry so about the things
of this world when so many mansions await you in the
world to come (see John 14:2)?

The Universal Choir

As if in response to the new song of the elders, a tre-   5:11
mendous chorus of exaltation erupts from every creature in heaven. The "angels around the throne and the
living creatures and the elders" all join in. The number
used to describe them is incalculable: "myriads of myriads, and thousands of thousands." These too, cry out,
"Worthy is the Lamb...," for He has been slain and
has risen to reign.

Notice that there are seven expressions of praise used   5:12

in this doxology, serving as a heavenly affirmation of the perfections and deity of the Lamb. He is worthy of power, riches, wisdom, might, honor, glory, and blessing. As if the heavenly choir were not enough to express the honor due the Lamb who has overcome, "every created thing" in the universe joins in the chorus. This final addition to the song of praise ascribes equal "blessing and honor and glory and dominion" both to 5:13,14 "Him who sits on the throne, and to the Lamb." Here again we see the unity and intimacy of the Father and Son, indicating the full deity of Christ.

The four expressions of worship in this last chorus represent the universal aspect of the obeisance rightly due the Lord of all of creation, as the living creatures and elders continue their ceaseless adoration. It is incredible that while in this vision we see all creation doing homage to the Son, millions of men and women in this world, created in His image, refuse to bow their knees. Every person will one day find out who He is and will indeed kneel before Him (see Phil. 2:10,11). The question remains: Will we bow to Him now willingly, or on the last day under compulsion—when it is too late?

Two Contrasts

There are, then, two major contrasts between the heavenly scene we have just observed and the world in which we find ourselves today. First we have seen that true strength is often disguised in robes of apparent weakness. We must be careful not to fall for the power plays of this world which would hope to overcome us, dragging us into participation in its antichrist system. Instead, as Christians we must overcome the world by cultivating the kind of true strength which Jesus demonstrated on His way to the Cross: acting in love for the welfare of others, regardless of the personal cost. The world could certainly use more Christians with attitudes like that in these days of "looking out for number one."

The second contrast we have observed is a bit more subtle, but just as serious. This is the contrast between the praise afforded the Lord by the creatures in His presence and those of us still here on planet earth. True worship and praise of God can scarcely be found in our modern churches or in our individual lives. Perhaps that is because we haven't seen the Lord as He truly is.

In any case, when we leave this world to stand in the presence of the One who sits upon the throne and of the Lamb, we will be participating in quite a bit of honest-to-goodness worship. It might not hurt to begin practicing for that great day here and now, for to really know God is to worship Him, just as to know Him is eternal life. If you and I desire to gain the latter, we're going to have to learn to offer the former.

As we progressively are conformed to the image of the Lamb, humbly obedient to the revealed will of God—and as we learn to render true worship to the triune God of the Universe—we demonstrate our true grasp of the secret of strength. As the submissive Lamb turns out to be the conquering Lion, so as we participate in His "weakness" we share in His eternal victory. The submissive Lamb turns out to be the conquering Lion, and as we participate in His "weakness"—submission to the Father—we share in His strength and His eternal victory.

4. The Envelope, Please

The nominees have been announced, the secret vote has been counted, and the audience awaits with anticipation the revealing of the name of the Oscar winner. The master of ceremonies turns to his assistant and solemnly calls out, "The envelope, please." With the breaking of the envelope's seal and the reading of its contents, the watching world knows of the new winner of the Academy Award. So it is with the seven seals of the Revelation. As they are broken, God's hitherto secret plan is unfolded before us.

The Last Days and You

Before looking into the opening of the seven seals, let's make sure we properly understand the meaning of this phrase, "the last days." Surely if we are going to interpret rightly what God has planned for the last days, as recorded in Revelation 6, it will be important for us to understand what the Bible means by the term.

Have you always thought that the last days were limited to some time in the distant and misty future? Has thinking of the future been generally frightening to you? What does the Bible actually mean by this cryptic phrase, the last days? When are they, anyway? What if I were to show you that the Bible tells us the last days are now?

In Acts 2, Peter preaches what has become one of the most famous sermons of history, the sermon on the Day

of Pentecost. As he begins his homily, Peter, under the
anointing of the Holy Spirit, insists the supernatural
events which have taken place that day are in fulfillment of ancient prophecy. In fact, he quotes from the
prophet Joel: "... This is what was spoken of through
the prophet Joel: 'And it shall be in the last days,'
God says, 'That I will pour forth of My Spirit upon
all mankind...'" (vv. 16,17). In other words, Peter believes that the events of the Day of Pentecost have set
in motion the time in the history of the world known as
the last days. Remember—Peter spoke these words in
the first century.

The writer of the Epistle to the Hebrews makes the
same point when he opens his letter, "God, after He
spoke long ago to the fathers in the prophets in many
portions and in many ways, in these last days has spoken to us in His Son..." (1:1). The apostle John makes
the point that the last times had already begun in the
first century when he writes, "Children, it is the last
hour; and just as you heard that antichrist is coming,
even now many antichrists have arisen; from this we
know that it is the last hour" (1 John 2:18).

The point is, the last days, biblically understood, began in the first century with the death, resurrection,
and ascension of Jesus, and the giving of the Holy Spirit. This means that what we call church history is what
Scripture calls the latter days. We find that the Book of
Revelation, written about those last days, is relevant to
us here and now. Regardless of how we may count time,
God says the coming of the Messiah has inaugurated the
last days of this world.

What does all of this have to do with the opening of
the seals in the Revelation? If we understand what the
Bible means when it talks about the last days, and if
we see that the opening of these seals unfolds the conditions permeating the world in the last days, we realize that the seals are not talking about some time off in
the future. They are describing the world as it is

today—as it has been since the time of Christ, and as it
will be until the end of the world. Therefore, the meanings of the seven seals are of importance to you and me
as believers today.

The First Seal: Nation Versus Nation

The first four of the seven seals form a unified group   **6:1**
in meaning, although we will consider them one by
one. When the first seal is broken, a crowned figure   **6:2**
appears riding on a white horse and carrying a bow,
and he goes out "conquering and to conquer." This figure offers us a picture of warfare which, in the first
century, was represented by the bow. The conquering of
one nation by another and the forceful subjugation of
one people to another was as common then as it is
today. This type of imperialistic conquest, also indicated by the crown on this rider's head, is to be characteristic of the last days. Even a cursory reading of world
history shows us this is true.

The Second Seal: Cain and Abel Revisited

The opening of the second seal brings forth a red
horse whose rider is permitted to take peace from the   **6:3,4**
earth and to cause men to kill one another. This rider
represents the bloodshed of warfare—not merely the
conquering of nations, but the killing of men which
accompanies such victories. So far is man from observ-
ing God's commandment to love one another that he
slays his fellow man. The first man born on this planet
killed his brother, and apparently the human race has
not improved much since that day of death. Instead of
learning how to live in peace with others, we have only
learned of more sophisticated and efficient methods to
destroy.

In the tumultuous arena of our twenty-first-century world it is not difficult to find fulfillments of the prophecies of these first two seals. Since the end of World War II, for example, godless dictators and blood-thirsty terrorists have tortured and killed untold thousands of innocent people. Recent events in Iran, Afghanistan, the Middle East in general, and numerous nations in Africa supply ample testimony of man's inhumanity to man. Spiritual as well as political cancer is certainly evidenced by the conquest and bloodshed of this age.

As Jesus describes this age in which we live, He points out that "you will be hearing of wars and rumors of wars" and that "nation will rise against nation, and kingdom against kingdom...But," He said, "all these things are merely the beginning..."(Matt 24:6–8).

Such international upheavals as we see today are not necessarily signs of the end of the world. Instead, as these first two seals indicate, they are characteristic of the last days in general, the whole period between the first and second comings of Christ. As followers of Christ in this violent, war-weary world, we should not be surprised by the conflicts brewing and breathing out around us.

Through the mysteries of the first two seals the Lord has told us that these things will come. But He is still the Sovereign One; He is still in charge. Though we may be disturbed by the evening news, we should be comforted by our knowledge that all authority in heaven and *on the earth* is Christ's. Though His rule may be often inscrutable to us, His perfect plan for the ages is being carried out to the letter. There are no accidents, international nor personal, in the providential reign of Jesus. Whether the conflict which troubles you takes place in the Middle East, in Washington, D.C., in your neighborhood, at work, or in the recesses of your own heart, remember that our Lord Jesus Christ is in control!

The Third Seal: Economic Chaos

The breaking of the third seal is marked by the ap-   **6:5,6**
pearance of a rider on a black horse. He has a pair of
scales in his hand. This specter represents economic
problems, scarcity of essential products, and uneven
distribution of wealth. A voice is heard with the emerg-
ing of this figure, "A quart of wheat for a denarius, and
three quarts of barley for a denarius; and do not harm
the oil and the wine." What is all of this about?

The denarius represented the normal daily wage for
a worker in the first century, and a quart of wheat
composed what was generally considered to be a daily
ration of food. A family man might have had to buy a
cheaper grain, such as barley, to feed his children, because he could get three quarts for the same price as
only one quart of wheat. The message of this seal is
that the last days will be typified by economic tensions.
A man will have to work all day just to get enough food
to feed himself and his family. Many people will live
"hand to mouth."

But then we read, "Do not harm the oil and the wine."
What could that mean? I believe these two products, oil
and wine, represent the types of commodities which
are enjoyed only by the wealthy—and they are "not
harmed." In other words, while the poor struggle to
earn their daily bread, the wealthy remain unscathed:
The rich get richer, and the poor get poorer. This is the
situation described by the third seal.

It is not difficult in today's worldwide inflationary
economy to see an example of this seal's fulfillment. Do
you find that you are required to live more and more on
less and less? Or perhaps you are wealthy. Though you
have had to cut back on some luxuries of late, your
basic standard of living is not in danger. Whichever
you are, remember your biblical responsibilities as a
Christian are to be obedient to God and sensitive to the

needs of others. Whether the Lord has prospered you materially or not, He requires you to use what you do have obediently and cheerfully for the advancement of His kingdom and the welfare of your brothers and sisters in Christ.

The Fourth Seal: The Grim Reaper

The breaking of the fourth seal calls forth a pale horse bearing a rider named "Death." Hades, the abode of the dead, is following close behind. There is power **6:7,8** given to them to bring about the demise of a significant minority of the population of the earth. What does this strange image signify?

Look at the figures associated with this fourth seal. They represent all of the various forms of death which strike men and women in this world, particularly those of an accidental or unexpected kind. In the first century, modes of death such as perishing by the sword, famine, pestilence, and attack by wild animals were not uncommon. Whoever expects to be killed by a wild animal? Who can predict the coming of a sudden famine? No man can predict or control such calamities.

If John had written the Book of Revelation in our time, he might have included in his list death by automobile accident, by heart attack, and by plane crash; through technology we have invented numerous new ways to kill ourselves. The point is: During the last days men and women will be dying from all sorts of unexpected causes, but that does not mean that God has forgotten about us or that He has lost control. Rather, the fact He has foretold these things by His apostle John confirms that He is still on the throne.

Have you lost someone close to you very suddenly and unexpectedly? I have. But I know that God is still God and that He has a plan which is being worked out perfectly. I don't always understand what His plan is.

But I know God is good and is working out His plan in my life.

A seven-year-old girl who is very dear to me recently faced her first Christmas without her father, who had died. A friend visiting the family commented on what a sad Christmas it was going to be. Lara replied, "Not for my dad. He's going to spend Jesus' birthday with Him!" That childlike (and very true) perspective is one we all need. That is the kind of faith which qualifies us to be overcomers.

The World We Live In

As you look back over these first four seals, ask yourself these questions:
- When do we find the things described by the opening of these seals taking place?
- When is it that nation has risen up against nation to bring one another under subjugation?
- When is it that men have killed one another for selfish purposes?
- When is it that there have been economic crises and imbalances in wealth and position?
- When is it that death has come to men unexpectedly, without warning?

Are such questions to be answered only by looking off into some future time because they cannot be accounted for in this age? Not at all. The events described in seals one through four have been characteristic of the entire period of the latter days. We have experienced these very things in our lifetime as have believers throughout the centuries.

These prophetic scriptures show us how the last days are here and now. Further, the Bible assures us that however gloomy today's outlook for the world might be, there is a happy ending to come. God has told us in advance not only that our problems would be difficult, but also that He is still the Sovereign. Through Christ we overcome, not by sidestepping all our problems but by persevering in the midst of them. Although world events may easily grow beyond our abilities to deal with them effectively, nothing is too hard for the Lord. The Book of Revelation teaches us that God controls the affairs of people. If He can successfully handle all of the great crises of the nations, surely He can show you the way of escape from personal difficulties as well.

The Fifth Seal: A Heavenly View

The fifth seal is quite different from the first four. **6:9** The scene in the opening of this seal shifts from the earth to heaven, where we find the souls of men and women who have been martyred for their faith in Jesus under the altar of the heavenly temple. These people are crying out for the righteous and just judgment of **6:10** God to fall upon the wicked, Christ-hating world that **6:11** put them to death. They are told that God will indeed bring about such a judgment, but that the time for it has not yet come. There are still more of His people whom the Father has singled out to be privileged to die for the faith. Being called upon to lay down one's life for Christ was considered to be the highest honor among the early Christians.

How different is this biblical attitude toward martyrdom from that of most believers today! It seems that the goal of most of God's people is to avoid offending or embarrassing others at all costs, even if it means offending God in the process. How long has it been since you were the object of even a dissenting comment because of your stand for Jesus Christ, let alone having your life threatened because of it? in the early centuries of the Christian church, there was little fear of dying for the faith. The primary fear for many was that they might die for some reason other than their faith in Jesus.

From the breaking of the fifth seal there are at least three important principles to be learned. First, those who suffer for the sake of Christ are precious in His sight. Notice where the souls of the martyrs are to be found in this vision. They are under the altar in the heavenly temple, the place where the blood of the sacrifices to God would have run down. If you are called upon to suffer, even to lay down your life for Christ's sake, count it a privilege in which to rejoice, not as a terrible affliction. We in the Western church know so little of what it means to suffer for the sake of the gospel, while even at this moment many brothers and sisters in other parts of the world are in great tribulation because of the testimony of their faith.

Second, those who appear in the eyes of the world to be defeated are actually victors in the eyes of God. The martyrs receive the white robe of victory. God does not share the values of the world. The foolishness of God is wiser than the wisdom of men.

Third, there is a certain number of those whom God has ordained to be killed for the sake of the gospel. This means that the deaths of Christians on behalf of their Lord are not tragic, chance accidents which have no significance or meaning. They are carefully watched events, observed by the Lord Himself. God is in charge, even when it appears that He has forgotten. He is always mindful of you, His beloved child.

Now let's add another question to the ones we asked earlier. "When is it that people have given their lives for the sake of the gospel of Jesus, because of the testimony which they have maintained?" Again, the answer is the same: It has always been so, even from the earliest days of the New Testament church. The meaning of the fifth seal, like the first four, is applicable to the church during this entire age in which we live.

The Sixth Seal: Cosmic Cataclysm

The sixth seal presents quite a different story. Its opening obviously does *not* describe anything which the church has ever experienced throughout all of its history. The sixth seal describes the conclusion of history on this earth, the ultimate judgment. Put simply, the events described in the opening of the sixth seal depict the approach of the end of the world.

There are seven happenings which take place with the opening of this seal: 6:12, 17

1) A great earthquake shakes the world (see Ezek. 38:19,20).

2) The sun turns black (see Amos 5:20).

3) The moon becomes like blood (see Joel 2:31).

4) The stars of the sky fall to earth (Ezek. 32:7,8).

5) The sky itself splits apart (see Is. 34:4).

6) Every mountain and island is moved from its place (see Hos. 10:8).

7) People seek to hide themselves from the wrath of God (see Is. 2:10; Joel 2:11; Mal. 3:2).

These events in and of themselves are compelling evidences of the cataclysmic effects of the opening of this seal. But how do we know that this seal's opening describes the end of this world?

Virtually all of the events enumerated in the seven happenings of seal six are found in the Old Testament (and in some non-canonical ancient writings called the Apocrypha and the Pseudepigrapha) as images referring to the close of history. Because we in the twenty-first century find it understandably difficult to think with first-century Eastern minds, we very often find it difficult to decipher the meanings which were clear to the early believers to whom John wrote. They understood the sources for the imagery in the Book of Revelation were to be found in the Scriptures (what we know today as the Old Testament), not in tomorrow's headlines.

Thinking With a First-Century Mind

This is precisely how the meaning of the terrible images of the sixth seal become clear: by entering into the mindset of the original recipients of these visions, by seeing them through their eyes and understanding them through their minds. After all, this book is a revelation, not an "obscuring"! I believe our brothers and sisters to whom the Revelation was originally penned *did* understand its symbols, and so can we, if we "get inside their heads" by thinking in Old Testament concepts.

Holy Spirit or Fire?

The cosmic cataclysm of the sixth seal refers not only to the closing of this age. It also proclaims a sobering message to the unbelieving world: The time of reckoning when all people, whether great or small in the eyes of the world, must stand before God the Judge. The terror of that sudden but too-late realization is depicted in further imagery, also drawn from the Old Testament. The people of this world, from the emperor to the slave, seek to hide from the judgment of God, which they know is about to befall them. They hope the mountains and rocks will fall upon them, a calamity which most people would avoid at all costs. But having a mountain fall upon one is nothing compared to facing unprepared the holy justice of God's wrath as He makes recompense for unrepentance toward sin. The time for the coming of the holy anger of the Lamb has arrived; indeed, "Who is able to stand?"

Everyone who has ever lived will experience either the love of the Lamb or His wrath. As John the Baptist said, "He will baptize you with the Holy Spirit and fire" (Luke 3:16). Those who do not willingly receive the Holy Spirit by faith in Christ unwillingly will undergo the fiery judgment. There is no neutral ground; he who is not *for* the Lamb is *against* Him. When the great day

6:15

6:16

6:17

of His wrath is come, none who oppose Him will be able to stand.

If you are not certain of your standing in the eyes of the Lamb, He offers you Himself and His sacrifice right now. "... He who believes *has* eternal life" (John 6:47). Trust in the payment He made on the Cross for sin—or understand that you must make payment yourself on the Last Day.

144,000: Who Are They?

The question of earth's inhabitants—Who is able to stand in the day of the wrath of the Lamb?—is a reasonable one. Who will be able to stand uncondemned before our holy and just God? Will all be consumed in His just anger? This is the question which John now addresses as he tells of his vision of the 144,000.

The vision of Revelation 7 reveals the destiny of those 7:1 who have accepted the gospel of Christ, who are depending upon Him and His work on the Cross for their acceptance before God. They are not leaning upon their own supposed ability to please God by their own works, for they know that only perfection is acceptable to God—and only the work of Jesus is perfect.

Before the final judgment of the sixth seal is unleashed upon the earth, there are some who will be separated out to escape the destruction about to befall the peoples 7:3 of the earth. These are, according to Revelation 7, "the bond-servants of our God" who are "sealed ... on their foreheads." They are sealed before the anger of God falls upon the earth and the sea.

Who are these "sealed ones" who escape judgment? John tells us that he heard the number of those sealed, 7:4 "one hundred and forty-four thousand sealed from every tribe of the sons of Israel." If you had been among those first-century believers who first heard John's account of this vision, who would you have thought the 144,000 to be? Their identity has been a matter of discussion for centuries. Who are these "sons of Israel"?

The apostle Paul teaches it is not those who are descendants of Abraham according to the flesh who make up the true Israel. It is rather those who are *of faith* who are his children (see Gal. 3:7). "If you belong to Christ, then you are Abraham's offspring, heirs according to promise" (v. 29). John, in speaking of the 144,000, is not describing the citizens of the earthly or gathered nation of Israel; he is talking about those who are members of the spiritual Israel, Abraham's true and faithful family in the church.

144,000: The New Israel

This Book of Revelation becomes so much more real to me when I realize that by grace I am included in this multitude of 144,000. I am sealed, I am protected, I am loved. And if you belong to Christ, so are you! This becomes plain when we examine the list of the tribes in verses 5–8. As you read you will find that it is unlike any other list of the tribes found in the Bible. The tribe   **7:5–8** of Judah is mentioned first here, although it is never first in any Old Testament list. Why is that? It is because the Messiah, the Lion of Judah, hailed from that tribe, giving it a new preeminence.

You will also note that the tribe of Dan is not included. However, the tribe of Joseph, not mentioned in Old Testament lists, is included here. The half tribe of Ephraim is not included in Revelation; the half-tribe Manasseh, Joseph's other son, is listed. Levi is mentioned, though no land was given to that tribe of priests. This is thoroughly confusing if John is intending for us to get a picture of the tribes of old Israel. But that is the point: John does not mean for us to be thinking of visible Israel. This is a seal of the living God and it is set on *spiritual* Israel, that is, the church of Jesus Christ.   **7:2** We of the church are the ones who are protected from the judgment of God, for there is no condemnation for those who are in Christ Jesus (see Rom. 8:1). Since He has borne our judgment already, we need not fear the judgment to come.

The Secret Number of the Church

But what of this number, 144,000, about which so
many speculations have been made? To unlock this mystery, we must begin by realizing the significance of the
number itself: 144,000 is broken down easily into the
factors 12 × 12 × 1000. As we saw in the preceding chapter, *twelve* is a number which represents the church. We
observed that in the Old Testament, the people of God
existed in the twelve tribes of Israel. In the New Testament, the twelve apostles serve as the foundation
stones upon which the church is built. Thus we see the
connection between the number twelve and the church,
the people of God.

The number one thousand also has significant meaning in the Scripture. When we read that He owns "the
cattle on a thousand hills" (Ps. 50:10), for example, we
do not suppose that on hill number 1001, we can keep
all the cattle we find there since they do not belong to
God. Of course not! The phrase means He owns all
the cattle (and everything else) on every hill (and
everywhere else). The earth is the Lord's and all of
its fullness. The number one thousand is employed
by the psalmist to represent a wholeness or a totality.

The same is the case here in Revelation 7. The number 144,000 is the product of the number of the Old
Testament church (12) together with that of the New
Testament church (12) represented in their totality (1000).
Who are the ones sealed? They are the ones who have
trusted in the deliverance of the Lord. It is we who have
been "grafted in" to the vine (see Rom. 11:17–20) as well
as those believers from the natural sprig of physical
Israel—those both before and after the Cross—who comprise the true Israel of God. On the last day, we shall all
be there standing joyfully before the throne of the Lamb.
And John hears our blessed number: 144,000 from the
tribes of Israel.

Countless Christians

This comforting truth is confirmed when we notice   **7:9**
what happens next in this vision. After John hears the
number 144,000, he looks and sees the reality behind
it. He says, "...I looked, and behold, a great multitude,
which *no one could count,* from every nation and all
tribes and peoples and tongues..." (italics mine). God
is not concerned with a static and limited number, but
rather with a countless multitude. That vast sea of
people comes not only from the one nation, Israel, but
rather from every nation of the earth and from every
period of history. The 144,000 Israelites and the worldwide multitude are one and the same! They are the followers of the Lamb, the people of God, the church of
Jesus. If you belong to Christ, then you share in the
blessings of the countless multitude of 144,000.

Where is this group representing the church to be
found? They are standing before the throne of God and
of the Lamb. Here is the answer to the question posed
by the perishing world, "Who is able to stand?" The
church! Those of us who by grace have been purified by
the atonement of the Cross, are alone able to stand in
the holy judgment. The rest of the world is consumed.

Finally we observe the activity of this vast multi-   **7:10–**
tude. We are told that they continually cry out the   **12**
praises of God in the presence of the Lamb and of the
angels. When the question is asked concerning the
identity of these victors clothed in white, the answer is   **7:14**
that they are "the ones who come out [literally: "are
coming out"] of the great tribulation, and they have
washed their robes and made them white in the blood of
the Lamb."

From this we again observe that those who say that
the time of the Tribulation is entirely future are not
saying enough. We have already found in Revelation 1
that John describes himself as "a fellow partaker in the
tribulation" with the believers in the first century. The   **1:9**

church has been under attack throughout time and will be until the end, when Christ Himself shall vindicate the persecution His people have undergone.

The small troop of soldiers fighting an army obviously outnumbering them might easily be fearful and discouraged, and even surrender. But if that troop knows that an overwhelming force of allies is on the way to the battle scene, they will fight all the more courageously—not because they are currently winning the battle, but because they know that ultimate victory is assured. So it is with us.

The church has been under fire from its very inception. The world has been seeking the destruction of the people of God from the start. This truth might at first seem frightening. But in fact it is a great comfort to us believers. While it is true Jesus warned of tribulation in this world, He has also assured us that He has "overcome the world" (John 16:33). Let the world do what it will—the church of Christ is invincible! Hell cannot win against it. As Luther wrote so beautifully,

> *Let goods and kindred go,*
> *This mortal life also.*
> *The body they may kill;*
> *God's truth abideth still.*
> *His kingdom is forever.*

This blessed perspective is further affirmed by John's statement near the end of Revelation 7. "These are the **7:14** ones who [are coming] out of the great tribulation..." The 144,000, representing the church, through the centuries have gone through tribulation and have emerged victorious, because they have been identified with the victory of Christ over the Evil One and his power of death. The tribulation then can neither be entirely future not only of a limited end-time duration. "In the world you have tribulation," Jesus assured us, "but take courage; I have overcome the world" (John 16:33).

The blessings which fall upon us who overcome with   **7:15–17**
Him are great. These blessings are summarized in the
final verses of the seventh chapter, where we are promised
the eternal care of God.

Remember, if you belong to Jesus Christ, these verses
are written for and about you. What is your tribulation? Jesus knows all about it. What is your trial? He
has experienced it already and is ready to sustain you
whatever your problem may be. As a believer, as part of
the great multitude called the 144,000, you are sealed
into the love of Christ, the fellowship of the Holy Spirit,
and the eternal protection of the Father. What trouble
can stand before that awesome reality? You are loved by
Jesus, and no one can snatch you out of His hand (see
John 10:29).

The Seventh Seal: Eternal Peace

Now we encounter a problem. If the sixth seal represents the end of the world, then what could the seventh
seal possibly signify? To put it another way, what could
follow the end?

It is in asking the question in the latter form, that   **8:1**
the answer becomes apparent. That which follows the
end of this world is the beginning of the world to come.
This is what is indicated by the mysterious silence of
the seventh seal.

Following the great tumult and noise of the sixth
seal's events, the silence at the opening of seventh seal
is certainly arresting. This silence is of no brief duration. It lasts, in the vision, for a full half hour (remember that in terms of the vision's time frame, the whole
history of the world between the first and second comings has apparently occupied only a few minutes).

This lengthy silence at the opening of the seventh
seal is symbolic of the eternal peace that awaits those
who have endured the great tribulation of this world

and have overcome the world through Christ. The final seal, as it is broken, assures all of us who have made the Rock of Ages our refuge that the peace which this world has refused to give awaits us in the eternal kingdom He has prepared for us.

Summary of the Seals

The seven seals give us an overview of conditions which have been manifest since the birth of Christ and which will continue to be evident in this world until His second coming. I hope you are encouraged by the story told by the seals. Through them we are assured that although the battles in this world will not be easy, God is always in control of the circumstances. He has prepared a glorious future for us, as we persevere in faith and good works until the end.

In the final reckoning it is not those who are especially strong or gifted or beautiful or clever or wealthy or influential who are blessed of God. Often even believers adopt the world's perspectives and find themselves envying those who possess such qualities, coveting the things which worldly wisdom values. The comfort of the seven seals is the assurance that it is those of us who belong to Christ—even though we may be called upon to suffer here and now—who will enjoy the fruitful blessings of God throughout all eternity. It is this assurance which makes the good news so good!

5. Facing the Music

When you think of the sound of a trumpet and the music it makes, what comes to your mind? Perhaps it's the music of the Canadian Brass or Wynton Marsalis, happy and mellow sounds which put your mind at ease. Throughout most of modern history the sound of the trumpet, and music in general, has been closely associated with entertainment, relaxation, and good times.

But in ancient days the sound of the trumpet had quite a different meaning. Its blast sounded *warning*, warning of an approaching danger or an attacking enemy. For this reason, when the trumpets of God are sounded in the Book of Revelation, no one thinks of dancing. Through the blowing of these trumpets the warning of impending judgment is proclaimed throughout the earth. Men and women are called once again by the Lord Jesus Christ to turn from their rebellion against Him and to God for deliverance.

Regarding the trumpets, two questions arise: When are they blown, and what does each trumpet specifically signify? The answers to these questions will make up the bulk of this chapter.

The Trumpets Are Sounding Today

In the last chapter we saw how the meaning of the seals can be applied properly to you and me and the world we live in today. Exactly the same thing is true of the trumpets. The sounding of these instruments represents God's activity in the world today, and they display the balance of His perfect plan for the age. This means, of course, that the message of the trumpets is relevant to you, to warn or to encourage, according to your need.

Seven Angels Plus One

The trumpets which are blown in Revelation 8 are held by seven angels standing before God, ready to do His will. These seven appear ready to sound their horns, but before any of the trumpets are blown another angel appears in front of the altar in heaven. This angel mixes incense with the fire of the altar and throws it down to the earth, causing great disturbance in the world. What do we make of this event? **8:2**

8:3–5

The purpose of the Book of Revelation, as we have noted, is to comfort and encourage believers like you and me who will go through difficult times because of faith in Jesus Christ. Ever since the first appearance of the Messiah, Christ's people have been praying for His return, for their own salvation, and for the destruction of the evil world-system which seeks to choke out all forms of godliness and faith. Yet, though we pray for these things, it is sometimes very difficult to believe they will actually come about. Because of the cancerous growth of wickedness and man's self-centeredness, and due to the daily struggles we face, questions arise. Does God *really* hear my prayers? Why doesn't He do something?

The vision described at the beginning of Revelation 8 is a reminder to you as a child of the King that He does hear your prayers, and that He has not forgotten them—nor you. We saw earlier the martyrs under the altar, praying for the avenging of their blood and being told to wait a little longer for God's perfect justice. So here, too, we are reminded that God is working out a plan largely unknown to us. We must be patient, realizing His ways are often beyond our understanding. As **6:9–11**

a matter of fact, God's partial judgment upon the unbelieving world which takes place now, during this age, is
largely in response to the prayers of Christ's church.
Hence we see the incense of our prayers being mixed with
the fire of His judgment before being cast down upon the
rebellious world.

It is important to remember that the judgments of
God laid upon this world are intended as a means of
both calling men and women to repentance and punishing
sin. The patience of God, even with those who rebel
against Him, is great, and we as His people should be
no less loving and longsuffering than He.

What about the neighbor who has criticized you? How
about your ex-friend to whom you're too proud to apol-
ogize? Have you been out of touch with your husband or
wife because of your lack of forgiveness? Jesus said that
if we do not forgive others, the Father will not forgive
us (see Matt. 6:15). Perhaps it's time for you to erase
some long-standing accounts, to get right with some
other people and with God. Though He will destroy the
unbelieving world on the Last Day, He is waiting now
for men and women to be reconciled to Him.

The First Four Trumpets

When we studied the opening of the first four seals,
we saw that they revealed what God would be doing
during this age to emphasize to men their need for Him
and His direction in their lives. Those first four seals,
represented by the four horsemen, are a unit, each
depicting one aspect of the multifaceted activity of Christ
in the world.

The same thing can be said of the first four trumpets.
Their meaning is also applicable to us who live in the
current age, and they are rightly understood as a unit.
Each of these trumpet judgments affects a different part
of the creation, and these first four all derive their
imagery from a familiar story from the Old Testament.

The First Trumpet: Effects on the Land

As the first trumpet is blown "hail and fire, mixed   **8:7**
with blood" is thrown down to the earth. As this great
storm buffets the earth, a third of everything on the dry
land, including the trees and the grass, is destroyed.
What is the significance of this terrifying storm?

In the history of God's people Israel, we read of a
number of plagues which the Lord brought upon the
unbelieving land of Egypt. Those judgments ultimately
resulted in the freedom of God's people from their bondage. One of the plagues given by God through the hand
of Moses was a plague of hail and fire, which virtually
destroyed the crops and thus the economy of the land.
(see Ex. 9:24). It is important to notice that the Bible
says while this storm was very severe upon the unbelievers of Egypt, it did not affect the believing Israelites
at all (see v. 26). While bringing judgment upon His
enemies, God protected His own.

This warning and promise is similarly the message
of the first trumpet of Revelation. Though life in this
present age may not be a bed of roses (roses *do* have
thorns), God will supernaturally protect and care for
you and all His sheep. On the other hand, those who
continue in insolent unbelief may expect the displeasure of God to remain upon them. The distraught unbeliever may ask, "Why me?" The trumpets sound out the
answer, "Because God wants you to turn in your affliction to Him at this moment, that you might escape the
eternal wrath to come."

What About the One Third?

Each of the first four trumpets is said to affect one
third of either the land, the sea, the rivers, or the sky.
The fraction is not intended to have a mathematical
meaning here, but rather an illustrative meaning rep-

resenting a *significant minority* of the earth. In other words, the judgment of God upon this world during this age is not total. The fullness of His wrath is reserved for the Last Day. Nevertheless, a man cannot sin without reaping the results of what he sows, even during this age. Thus one third, an incomplete yet significant portion of God's displeasure, will be meted out against those who oppose Him. This warning is the biblical version of the old saying, "Crime does not pay." Its truth is experienced even this side of the final judgment.

The Second Trumpet: The Effects on the Sea

The blowing of the second trumpet brings about judgment upon the sea and those things in it and on it. One third of the waters of the sea become blood, the living things in the sea die, and a third of the ships on the sea are destroyed. **8:8,9**

This second trumpet's judgment is also reminiscent of one of the plagues of the Exodus. You will recall the first of the plagues which God visited upon the Egyptians was the turning of the waters of the Nile into blood so that the fish in it died (see Ex.7:20). The water was unfit for any use. The Nile was and continues to be of supreme importance to the land of Egypt. In the time of Moses it was even worshipped by the Egyptians as a god. Thus the true and living God showed Himself to be far superior to the god of Egypt.

The same meaning is derived from this second trumpet. With its blowing, not merely a river but a whole sea turns to blood. For us the sea represents the expanse of salt water we call the oceans or the "seven seas." In the first-century world, it was the Mediterranean Sea that held the key to travel and commerce. This sea provided food as well as communication lines through the shipping trade.

Whether it be seven seas or one, God can destroy it all. Throughout this age, God has been seeking to re-

mind us of our finitude and our need for our Creator by
afflicting us on the sea as well as on the land. Such
troubles should cause us to seek God, but still men
harden their hearts against Him.

The Psalmist comforts us as children of the living
God by reminding us that "...we will not fear, though
the earth should change, and though the mountains
slip into the heart of the sea" (Ps. 46:2). Here is the
source of the image of the burning mountain cast into
the sea which is employed in the vision given to John.
It is a reminder once more of Christ's care for us. Even
when the most terrible events of history befall the world,
there is protection for those who trust in Him. Even
when this "great mountain" is thrown into the sea,
there is still no cause for alarm for believers in Jesus
Christ.

The Third Trumpet: Effects on the Rivers

The third trumpet, when it is sounded, also has an **8:10,**
effect upon the waters, in this case the rivers and springs, **11**
the sources of fresh water. Plainly, this type of water
was of great importance in the ancient world, for while
one could travel upon the great sea and catch fish from
its waters, no one could drink it. The fresh waters on
land were important for that use, and with the blowing
of this trumpet, one third of these waters is made bitter.

Mankind can live for an extended time without the
normal comforts of this world, for many days even without food, but no one can go long without water. When
water becomes undrinkable, life is severely threatened.
Here is the hard meaning of the blowing of the third
trumpet. In order to evoke the repentance of men, God
will bring about conditions where life is endangered, in
order that people will call upon Him. He has been doing
this since the beginning of the age, and in His mercy
He will continue to do so until the end. Such judgments
of the Lord upon unbelievers are actually acts of mercy,

as He calls out to get their attention and impress upon them their need of Christ.

This pollution of the rivers and springs is similar to the plague already discussed, when the Nile was rendered useless to make Pharaoh repent (see Ex. 7:19, 24). But there is another story associated with the Exodus that is important in rightly understanding this symbol from the Revelation.

After the Israelites had fled Egypt and crossed the Red Sea, they ran short of water in the wilderness (see Ex. 15:23–25). They finally discovered an oasis named Marah, but the water there was bitter and undrinkable. God miraculously turned that bitter water into sweet for the welfare of His people. Thus we have an interesting contrast: For those who love Him, God will make the bitter sweet. For those who resist and reject Him, He makes the sweet bitter. Once again we see at work the principle that we who trust in the Lord Jesus Christ can be comforted with the assurance of His care, while those who ignore His claims upon them face bitter judgment.

The Fourth Trumpet: Effects on the Sky

The sounding of the fourth trumpet affects the sky   8:12
rather than any portion of the earth itself. Once more it is one third of creation which is disturbed. The sun, the moon, and the stars are darkened.

This trumpet also derives its imagery from the plagues sent upon Egypt before the Exodus. "Moses stretched out his hand toward the sky, and there was thick darkness in all the land of Egypt for three days." (Ex. 10:22). In order to free his people and to soften the hardened hearts of Pharaoh and his followers, the Lord caused the luminaries of the heavens to be blotted out, no longer sending their light to the earth.

In a similar way, God withholds His light from those who continue to rebel against Him. Why is it that such rebels in today's world, even those with wealth and fame and influence, do not derive lasting satisfaction from their achievements? It is because God will not allow it. Things which He has not blessed, things which are not set apart for His glory, will never meet the needs of men.

Notice, however, what the Exodus passage has to say about the homes of the believing Israelites during the plague of darkness: "... all the sons of Israel had light in their dwellings" (10:23). Pharaoh may have had a beautiful palace, but he could not enjoy it because of the darkness which surrounded him. Yet the humble nation under the rule of Jehovah had light because of His presence. Is it any wonder Jesus is called the light of the world (see John 8:12), that in Him is no darkness at all (see 1 John 1:5)?

The message of the first four trumpets, then, is that during this age the judgment of God upon the unrepentant and unbelieving will be manifested in many ways. Wherever we may be we cannot escape the scrutiny and the justice of God. But if you have softened your heart and turned to Christ, you have become one of the blessed ones who are sustained through the difficulties and trials which are a part of life in a fallen world. The severity and the mercy of God are plainly seen through the first four of the seven trumpets.

The Warning of the Vulture

Before the fifth angel places his trumpet to his lips, **8:13** John envisions a vulture (or "eagle"; the word is the same in the Greek) crying out a solemn warning to "those who dwell on the earth." (Remember that the phrase "those who dwell upon the earth" represents the unbelievers of this world, whose dwelling place is here below rather than above with Christ.) The next three trumpets will provoke more terrible judgments against the world, and so three "woes" are spoken on behalf of those who will experience them. Here is a warning to flee from the wrath of God by fleeing to His mercy.

The Fifth Trumpet: The Locusts From the Pit

With the blowing of the fifth trumpet, truly terrible images are employed to represent the intensified warnings which God sends out into the world as the Last Day approaches.

The "star from heaven which had fallen to the earth" **9:1** represents Satan. (Jesus said, "I was watching Satan fall from heaven like lightning" [Luke 10:18].)

Notice Satan is given the key to the bottomless pit. The whole universe, including even the power of evil, is under the control of God Almighty. Yet, it must be understood clearly that God is not the author of evil (see James 1:13). If the Evil One is to do any of his dastardly work, he may do so only with permission from the Father. The myth that Satan is "the king of hell" is just that: a myth. As a matter of fact, Satan will be hell's chief prisoner on the Last Day when he is cast into the lake of fire. The comfort for you and me comes from knowing that evil is never autonomous to do its own thing. Even the evil things which befall us must pass the scrutiny of the Father.

In this vision, John sees the Devil opening up a cav- **9:2,3** ernous pit, out of which comes a gigantic cloud of locusts. These locusts are hideous in their appearance, and it is plain that they do not represent any normal earthly creatures. What could such a horrible vision signify, and what does it mean to us today? Scripture itself gives us the interpretation.

Once again we turn to the story of the Exodus. We read there of a plague of locusts sent upon Egypt (see Ex. 10:12–15). Those locusts totally covered the land and devoured every living plant in sight. The locusts of the Revelation also cover the whole earth, but curiously they do not harm the plants of the earth. They attack men.

But notice which men are susceptible to their sting: It is those "who do not have the seal of God on their **9:4** foreheads." In other words, these locusts are used of God to torment those who continue to reject the free offer of forgiveness and eternal life through Christ.

The Five Months

We are told that these locusts are permitted to tor- **9:5** ment the unbelieving world for five months. What does this time period signify? These torments upon men do not comprise the final judgment, being of limited duration. They are rather those pains of life which are always entering into the experience of men and women who do not know Christ.

Further, the five months may well be a reference to the 150 days during which the water stayed upon the earth in the time of the Flood (see Gen. 7:24). That flood was a worldwide judgment. There was no place one could go to escape, except into the ark of Noah. Similarly, during the five months or 150 days of the locusts' torment, there is no place to hide save in the grace of Jesus Christ. If one was not in the ark, then he necessarily drowned in the Flood, and if one is not in Christ, then he necessarily sinks under the judgment of God.

The Locusts' Appearance

The bizarre appearance of these locusts is derived **9:7–** from the prophecy of Joel, who describes the desolation **10** of an unbelieving and disobedient land by a plague of locusts (Joel 1,2). Using precisely the same descriptions as in the Revelation, Joel points out that the judgment of

God can be avoided by turning in repentance to the Lord (see 2:12,13).

Terrible pains and misfortunes are the lot of those who continue to go their own way, for like a plague of locusts the curse of God upon His enemies covers the earth. The king over the locusts is called "Abaddon" (in **9:11** Hebrew) or "Apollyon" (the Greek name). Both these names mean "destruction." The "angel of the abyss"—the Devil himself, the "destroyer"—has sway over those who do not display the brand of God upon their foreheads. They bear instead the mark of the Beast, the Evil One. Just as believers are marked and thus owned by God, so unbelievers are branded and belong to the destroyer.

The Sixth Trumpet: Angels at the Euphrates

With the blowing of the sixth trumpet, the judgment **9:13–15** of God against unbelief becomes even more intense. Four angels are released "that they might kill a third of mankind." These angels, we are told, had been bound at the Euphrates River awaiting the precise moment for their activity to begin. What should we understand from this vision?

First of all, the fact that there are four angels who go forth indicates the worldwide impact of their deadly work, for they go to the four corners of the earth or to the four points of the compass. As we have already seen, *four* is the number used to represent the vastness of creation. In this case, the number can be understood in terms of the universality of judgment.

Second, these angels are "bound at the great river Euphrates" as they await their release. In the ancient world, the Euphrates was considered to be the boundary between East and West. The Euphrates was the eastern boundary of the land that God promised to the descendants of Abraham (see Gen. 15:18). In other words, the Bible says this river is the ideal border of the land of Israel. Anything "beyond the Euphrates" is outside the church and beyond the realm of the experience of true believers. When these four angels are released, they do not attack Christians but the unbelieving world, and wherever they go they take death and its accompanying sorrows and pain.

Again, the fraction one third is used to designate the extent of their influence. But as they go, they go only at the "hour and day and month and year" for which they have been prepared. Even death does not go forth into the world of its own accord but rather under the counselled plan of God. Once again we observe the tender care of Christ for His church. Even though the world may fall, His kingdom is forever, and all of His people are secure.

The Multitude of Horsemen

Along with the release of the four angels, a tremendous number of "horsemen" go forth. These riders and their horses are fantastic in their appearance. Plainly, they are no earthly creatures. These horsemen represent the demonic army which is loosed upon the unbelieving world to do it harm, so that some might repent and turn to the salvation which is in Christ. They have heads like lions and tails like snakes (animals often are used in the Bible as representations of the Evil One [see 1 Pet. 5:8]). These horsemen are demonic entities, released into the world to torment and even kill so that the sinful human race might turn to Christ. **9:16, 17** **9:18, 19**

But note something here. Instead of thanking God for sparing them, those who are not killed by these evil creatures, continue to turn to false gods and reject Christ. By this time the patience of God is nearly spent. **9:20, 21**

The First Six Trumpets: A Look Back

In the blowing of the first six trumpets we have seen the representations of the various warnings and partial judgments which Christ is visiting upon the world during this present age. All of creation has been affected by the displeasure of God toward sin, men themselves most of all. God's patience allows men to continue to live even after they rebel against Him, but instead of being grateful for His mercy, they use it as an opportunity to sin all the more. Even when God brings about death and destruction, people will neither fear God nor turn from their self-will and idolatry to Him. Since they refuse God's mercy, nothing then is left except the terrors of the final judgment on the Last Day, represented in the blowing of the seventh trumpet.

The Strong Angel and the Little Book

Before the blowing of that last trumpet, however, an interlude in the vision confirms that which we have seen already. In a vision rich in Old Testament imagery we are told of the worldwide spread of the gospel both to those who will believe and to those who will reject it.

Revelation 10 depicts a "strong angel" coming to the **10:1,2** earth with an open book in his hand. This book is the Word of God, with the message of salvation in Christ on every page. This enormous angelic giant straddles the earth and the sea as he stands holding the book. Here the gospel is represented in its universal power and significance. All people on the earth and on the sea must hear it and heed it if they are to escape the Day of Judgment which is to come.

The Seven Peals of Thunder

But before the angel can speak to John, "seven peals   **10:3,4**
of thunder uttered their voices." Then, just as John is
about to write down what the peals of thunder have
revealed, he is prevented from doing so. Consequently,
no one knows what the thunders mean or what they
said. But perhaps that is the point: Lest we as humans,
even believing men and women, think that we have all
of the answers and understand everything about God's
plan, we should recall the mystery of seven thunders.
There is much to the gospel which we can understand,
but there is much, much more to the eternal plan of
God than we can ever imagine. These mysterious peals
of thunder remind us that we do not know all.

After the roar of the thunder has quieted, the angel   **10:5–7**
swears by the Creator Himself that there shall be no
more delay. With the sounding of the seventh trumpet,
"the mystery of God is finished" and the world comes to
its end.

The Bittersweet Gospel

Now a curious thing happens. John is told to take the   **10:8–**
book out of the angel's hand and to eat it. The angel   **11**
tells him that although it will taste sweet in his mouth,
it will make his stomach bitter. This imagery is drawn
from Ezekiel (see 3:1–3), as that prophet also was required
to eat a scroll full of the Word of God, with similar
effects on his mouth and stomach. What does all of this
mean?

The book held by the angel, as we have said, represents the gospel. When someone like Ezekiel or John,
or, for that matter, like you or me, takes the gospel
upon his lips to share it with another, it is indeed sweet.
Christians who have led others to faith in Jesus Christ

have experienced what is perhaps the greatest blessing available on this earth.

But there are also bitter consequences to the gospel. Because of that witness, multitudes in John's day and many today have been imprisoned, tortured, or killed. Sharing the gospel is a sweet task which you have as a Christian, but the results are often bitter. And we must soberly acknowledge this.

Measuring the Temple

The beginning of Revelation 11 depicts an event in John's vision which is very similar to another happening in Ezekiel's prophecy (see Ezek. 40–42). John, like Ezekiel before him, is commanded to "measure the temple of God, and the altar, and those who worship in it." What is meant by this newly offered command; what is this temple; and who are those who worship in it? **11:1**

In order to understand this vision, we must again remember the distinct functions of the Old and the New Testaments. The Old Testament contains pictures of truth which were shadows of realities which are made plain in the fullness of New Testament revelation. For example, the blood sacrifices under the old covenant can only be properly understood in light of the final sacrifice of Jesus on the Cross for sin, made once for all. The Old Testament rituals prepared the way for our understanding of the fullness of New Testament truth.

The temple in the Old Testament is just such a picture. The Jerusalem temple was the special covenantal dwelling place of God among His people. It was the place where believers could approach the Lord through the blood of the covenant sacrifices. The temple was the center of praise and worship, where the Holy Spirit of Jehovah made His abode.

Today there is no temple in Jerusalem or anywhere else, and there never will be another comparable to that of the Old Testament times. God is building a different kind of temple which replaces the old one, a new dwelling place for His Spirit where He is to be worshipped and praised and where He may be approached through His covenant. Where is that new temple? Or perhaps it is best to ask, *what* it is?

The answer to that question is plain in the New Testament. God will not cause a physical, material, earthly temple to be constructed again, for He is building His new dwelling place to last for all eternity. The new temple is a spiritual and heavenly one and although it is for a time imperfectly seen in this world, it is being built for the world to come. This new dwelling place of God is nothing other than the church, made up of believers in Jesus Christ, those who are indeed the dwelling places of God the Holy Spirit.

Listen to the apostle Paul: "Do you not know that you are a temple of God, and that the Spirit of God dwells in you?... The temple of God is holy, and that is what you are" (1 Cor. 3:16,17). Again, in speaking of the church of Jesus Christ, he says, "...the whole building [the church], being fitted together is growing into a holy temple in the Lord; in whom you also are being built together into a dwelling of God in the Spirit" (Eph. 2:21, 22).

Yes, it is the people of Christ who make up the new and spiritual temple, and it is this temple to which John refers in Revelation 11. He is to measure it for God—indicating God's watchful concern for all of the **11:2** intricate details of the lives and deaths of us who belong to Jesus—but he is to "leave out the court which is outside the temple" from his measuring. This outer court represents the unbelieving world who have been rejected by God, as they rejected Him. "It has been given to the nations; and they will tread under foot the holy city for forty-two months." John is telling us that the temple of God during this age—that is, the church—will be under attack by the unbelieving world, represented in this vision as "the nations," those not among the cho-

sen of Jehovah. This attack, or "treading under foot,"
will last for a period of forty-two months.

The Forty-Two Months

Should we look to the future anticipating a time period of forty-two months during which a special attack
will be made upon the people of God? Or could the
forty-two months be already past? Like the other images and numbers which are given in the Revelation,
we should understand that this forty-two months is spiritual, not statistical. Thus, the question remains as to
what the Holy Spirit is signifying by the figure.

This forty-two month period is mentioned in a number of other places in the Revelation, although it is
represented at times in different words. For example,
in the very next verse we read of a period of time called   **11:3**
the "twelve hundred and sixty days," which of course
equals forty-two months. This 1,260 days is also mentioned in Revelation 12, and the forty-two months is   **12:6**
referred to again in chapter 13. In addition, chapter 12   **13:5**
speaks of the "time and times and a half a time," or in   **12:14**
other words, three and a half times. This period is equivalent to three and a half years, according to ancient
usage—forty-two months or 1,260 days.

In other words, the Book of Revelation uses all of
these different ways of saying three and a half years
("forty-two months," "twelve hundred and sixty days,"
and "time and times and half a time") to represent
exactly the same period of time.

The question remains, however, as to what actual time
is represented by these phrases. I believe that those who
understand the forty-two months as being entirely future are forgetting some important history. A portion
of the forty-two months is, to be sure, yet to come, but the
characteristics of these 1,260 days have been evident in
the world since the time of Christ. As we examine the
happenings which are to take place during this time

span, we will see this period is emblematic of our entire interadvent age.

The Two Witnesses

We read of the appearance of the "two witnesses" who "will prophesy for twelve hundred and sixty days." When we discover what those two witnesses represent, then we will see that the 1,260 days represents the complete span of time from the first coming of Christ until his return at the end of the world.

But first, who are these two witnesses; or rather, what do they represent in this vision? Immediately following their introduction, the two witnesses are identified. We are told that they are "the two olive trees and   **11:4** the two lampstands." So now we know who they are—or do we? Before we can truly identify the two witnesses, we must find out what the olive tree and the lampstand represent.

This is not as difficult as it might first appear. In the Old Testament, the olive tree was often used as a symbol of Israel (see Ps. 52:8; Zech. 4). And as we have already seen from the early chapters of the Revelation itself, the lampstand signifies the church in the New Testament, the new Israel.   **1:20**

How long do these two witnesses make this proclamation? For "1,260 days," the entire interadvent period. And, of course, this is exactly what has been the case in the actual history of the church. Despite persecution and innumerable attempts to destroy Christ's church and the message it preaches, the Word of God and the people of God have continued to be manifest throughout history and around the globe. This truth should serve as a great encouragement to us today as we see the evil of the world exerting more and more influence in men's lives. Never forget that the gospel, too, gains influence over more and more lives each day, and that those of us who, like the two witnesses, participate in its propagation are assured of ultimate victory.

We are told that fire proceeds out of the mouths of **11:5** these two witnesses and that by this fire their enemies are overcome. This seems to be a rather bizarre picture until we realize that Jeremiah compares the Word of God in the mouths of His servants to fire which devours those who hear (see Jer. 5:14). All men will be devoured by the gospel, either being consumed by it through believing and embracing its truth or by being finally destroyed because of unbelief at the judgment of the Last Day. This is the eternal significance of the gospel, as it is proclaimed in this age by Christ's faithful witnesses.

Next we find that these two witnesses are compared **11:6** to Elijah and Moses, who stopped the sky from raining and smote the earth with various plagues, respectively. This comparison of the witnessing church to these great leaders is significant, for both Moses and Elijah fearlessly stood for the Word of God in the midst of severe opposition. Moses defied Egypt's Pharaoh, the most powerful sovereign of his day, and by the power of Jehovah overcame him and achieved release for the children of Israel. Elijah singlehandedly overthrew the corrupt and idolatrous worship of Ahab's Israel, defeating the prophets of Baal on Mount Carmel. The power of this world is nothing in the eyes of the Lord. If we are faithful to Him in our witness, He will bring about the downfall of the enemies of the Cross and, ultimately, our own victory. Can you honestly be numbered among those who are properly identified with these two witnesses?

Down to Defeat?

We next read something which is at first shocking **11:7** and totally unexpected: The two witnesses are killed! How can this be? The entire message of the Revelation is that there is ultimate victory for the church, the people of Christ.

While it is unthinkable that the church of Christ could be actually and totally destroyed, it certainly is imaginable that the church could be so suppressed by the evil forces of this world that its witness might be effectively *silenced* for a time. This silencing has in fact happened in various places throughout history, most notably in modern lands where the powers of atheistic communism and secular humanism have laid hold. Or, in its apostasy, the church is often said to be dead—still the church, but lifeless.

But we know that even in such cases the church is not gone, just sleeping. This is the meaning of the defeat and death of the two witnesses. From the world's perspective, the power of the Evil One ("the beast that comes up out of the abyss") has become so strong in the latter times that the church is wiped out, never to bother the world again with its annoying message of the need for repentance from sin and faith in Jesus Christ.

Thus the "great city which mystically is called Sodom **11:8** and Egypt, where also their Lord was crucified" rejoices at the thought of the annihilation of these pesky witnesses. This great city is the entire unbelieving world. Sodom, the place of immorality, and Egypt, the place of bondage, are apt symbols for the world which is controlled by the flesh and the Devil. Such a world has no time for "religious fanatics," such as the two witnesses. Men would just as soon not be reminded about the coming judgment of God and the claims of Christ upon them.

Indeed, while the remains of the witnesses lie in the **11:9,** midst of this great city of the world, its citizens declare **10** a holiday, sending gifts to one another in their joy, while heaping the ultimate contempt upon the witnesses by refusing them burial. It is almost humorous to note that "these two prophets tormented those who dwell on the earth." While the world may claim that the church is weak and of no effect, the fact is that even those who claim unbelief know that the message of God is true (see Rom. 1:18–21). Unbelievers are tormented by those who remind them of what they are so desperately trying to forget: The Holy Creator God is the One whom they will have to face.

The Two Witnesses' Triumph

The rejoicing of the unbelieving world is short-lived. **11:11** After three and a half days (note the similarity of this time period with that of Christ in the tomb) the witnesses rise from the dead. Here is the church of the Lord Jesus being manifested once more, but this time it is not to preach the word of salvation to the world. Now it is too late for those who have mocked at the message before, for the witnesses are taken up into heaven, even as **11:12** their enemies watch in confused terror.

Here is a picture of the resurrection of the saints on the Last Day. The true people of God from all ages (see 1 Thess. 4:16,17), here represented by the resurrected witnesses, will be caught up into the presence of God, while the world is left to receive the fullness of the judgment of God. "In that hour" of the deliverance of **11:13** the saints, the precursors of the final judgment have already begun. Immediately the seventh trumpet is **11:15** blown, signifying the close of the age.

The Seventh Trumpet: The End of the World

Jesus told us that He would "raise him up on the last day"—those who believed in Him for eternal life (see John 6:40). When we see, then, that Revelation 11 speaks of the taking up of believers into heaven, we know that the Last Day of the age is being described. Here we have the return of Christ for His own, the resurrection of all believers to meet Him, and the accompanying judgment of the unbelieving world.

This is precisely what takes place at the blowing of the seventh trumpet. As the final angel sounds the trumpet, the eternal reign of Christ is declared to have come in its final fullness. Though He has ruled since the time of His ascension, that rule was hidden from the eyes of the world. But on this last day, every knee shall bow and all shall acknowledge His kingship. A description of the last judgment is also given, as "the time came for the dead to be judged." Great reward is lavished upon those who have been faithful (that is, "full of faith"), and destruction is heaped upon those who have resisted and rebelled against Christ. The heavenly temple is opened to receive us, the church, triumphant at last, and the presence of the all-holy Lord of the Universe is signaled as it was on Mount Sinai of old, with the appearance of lightning and thunder and the quaking of the earth (see Ex. 19:16–18). **11:14–17** **11:18** **11:19**

As the vision of the trumpets is brought to a close, a great hope and encouragement is given to these who truly love Jesus. The promise of resurrection and future glory is ours. Whatever trials we may undergo in this world, they are not worthy to be compared with the glory to come. On the other hand, those who seek their glory in this world are duly warned that the day of wrath is rapidly approaching. When that day arrives, it will be too late for repentance. Today is the day of salvation: If you have salvation, share the good news. If you are not saved, the Lord Jesus Christ offers life freely to you right now, if you will trust in Him.

6. Good Guys and Bad Guys

Are you an old Western movie fan like I am? One of the fun things about those old flicks is how easy it always is to distinguish between the good guys and the bad guys. The good guys always seem to wear white hats, and the bad guys wear black ones. But as you have probably discovered by now, such simplicity exists only in the movies.

Just as true strength is frequently clothed in gentleness and seeming weakness, evil often wears the cloak of goodness. Jesus Himself warned us to beware of wolves in sheep's clothing, those who appear to be ministers of God but who are actually agents of the Evil One (see Matt.7:15). It is not always easy to distinguish the sheep from the wolves.

But in Revelation 12–14, the true identities of the actors upon the stage of the world are uncovered and their disguises are penetrated. These chapters speak of seven different characters, some good and some bad, who have major roles to play in the drama of this world's history. By understanding who they are and the parts they play, you and I can better interpret what is going on in the world today and what we can expect for tomorrow. More importantly, we can learn to trust more fully in the God who has prophesied these things to us, who is bringing all things to pass for His own glory and honor.

Chapters 12–14 comprise a single act in the drama; therefore they must be considered together. As in each of the other divisions of the Revelation, this one begins

its story with the inauguration of this present age, at
the time of the birth of the Messiah.

The Woman, the Dragon, and the Birth of Jesus

The scene beginning in Revelation 12 opens with a   **12:1,2**
picture of the incarnation of Christ. A woman, representing the Israel of the old covenant (which Hosea refers to as the wife of Jehovah [see Hos. 2:19,20]), is about
to give birth to a child. The woman wears a crown of
twelve stars, identifying her with the Old Testament
church. She is beginning her labor to bring forth a son,
the Messiah promised Israel according to Isaiah's prophecy (see Is. 9:6).

There is another figure who appears along with the   **12:3, 4**
woman. The great red dragon represents the Devil, the
serpent of old. The desire of the dragon is to kill the
Messiah as soon as He comes forth. You will recall that
at the birth of Jesus, Satan did indeed work through
Herod and the Roman armies in an attempt to kill the
baby Jesus.

This threat of the dragon signifies the war between
the serpent and the seed of the woman which was
prophesied in the Book of Genesis (see 3:15). That war
between the world (under the influence of Satan) and
the people of God (who belong to Christ) climaxes with
the advent of Jesus and the battle to the death which
He wages against Satan. That entire age-long war is
summarized in the first few verses of Revelation 12.

The whole life of Christ is summarized in just one   **12:5**
verse. We are told that the male child is born to rule
the nations, and that He is caught up to heaven to be
with God. Satan's attempts to frustrate the mission of
Christ fail; the Son fully satisfies the demands of the
Father and completes His work. He is thus received
into the presence of the Father. The entire life and
ministry of Jesus can be dealt with so summarily be-

cause that subject is not the primary concern of this vision. The purpose of the vision before us is to tell us of the fate of this woman, who is also under the attack of Satan.

God's Special Care for You

What of this woman, representing the church, who **12:6** must remain in a world which is under the influence of the Evil One? Is she forsaken and left on her own? No. She flees into the wilderness to a place specially prepared for her by God Himself, where she is cared for during a period of "one thousand two hundred and sixty days." In the last chapter we discussed the "forty-two months" and the "time and times and half a time," the entire period between the first and second comings of Jesus. We have in this chapter a beautiful picture of the church being cared for until Christ returns.

Today, during this period of strife for the people of Christ, you are under the blessing of God, but you are also subject to tribulation from the world. We found this to be true in the vision of Revelation 11, and we see it here again. God supernaturally cares for you in this world, but the Devil simultaneously is seeking to trip you up, to knock you down, and to destroy your testimony. You must beware of that roaring lion who seeks to devour you and learn to resist Him with Scripture as Jesus did.

The remainder of Revelation 12 describes in figura-   **12:13–1** tive language the attacks of Satan against the church during our "wilderness wanderings." Ancient Israel was freed from slavery in Egypt and was called into the Promised Land of Canaan, but before they were able to enter in they spent forty-two years in the wilderness.

We in the church have also been called out of bondage to sin and into the land promised us by God— heaven. But before we enter in, the church spends forty-two months in the wilderness of this evil world. During this time the dragon continues to be enraged with the woman and her children, that is, those "who keep the commandments of God and hold to the testimony of Jesus." The Scripture teaches that although the dragon is unrelenting in his attempts to destroy the woman, the church of Christ, God shall sustain us until the end.

Battle in Heaven

In the middle of chapter 12, we read the story of the war in heaven and the throwing down of Satan. This is not an easy passage to interpret, especially because of the mention of Michael and his angels doing battle with the armies of the Devil. This much is plain: The spiritual battle which is described in this passage has culminated with the defeat of Satan by Christ upon the Cross. The Devil is overcome "because of the blood of the Lamb."

Jesus prophetically saw this casting down of Satan **12:11** even before the Cross as He sent out His disciples to preach the gospel of the kingdom, and as He demonstrated His own authority over the demons (see Luke 10:17–20). Satan, being thrown down in defeat at the Cross, has become even more enraged against Christ and His people. Thus a warning is given to the earth and those who dwell on it: "Woe to the earth and the **12:12** sea, because the devil has come down to you, having great wrath, knowing that he has only a short time."

This "short time" is the period in which we now live. We should not be surprised, then, to see both the blessing and the tribulation of the church, for both God and Satan are now active in the world. The nature of Satan's activity has been much altered since his defeat on the Cross, but he is nevertheless a powerful adversary on "borrowed time" in the spiritual battle in which we are engaged.

Our problems, by the way, are not all the immediate

result of Satan's activities. Many of our troubles come as a response to our own sinfulness and ignoring God's Word. But the good news is that Jesus has overcome Satan's power and our sin so that we can be overcomers in both.

Man's Self-Exaltation: The Beast From the Sea

In the vision which John sees next there are a number of very strange images employed. If we are to understand them rightly, we must again enter into the minds of our first-century brothers and sisters in Christ to whom God originally gave this revelation, trying to discern what they understood concerning these figures. An important part of thinking as they did involves our own understanding of the prophetic writings of the Old Testament for, as we have seen time and again, the symbols seen in the Revelation are those also used by Daniel, Ezekiel, and other ancient prophets.

Revelation 13 tells us about two different beasts which **13:1,2** are extremely influential on the earth. One is a beast which is described as coming up "out of the sea," and the second beast is said to come up "out of the earth." **13:11** The beast from the sea is a hideous monster with seven heads and ten horns. Various parts of its body resemble a leopard, a bear, and a lion. Obviously this beast signifies something—but what? This is where an understanding of the visions of Daniel is so important (see Dan. 7:3–27).

Daniel had a vision of four beasts coming up out of the sea, each of which had characteristics of the one great beast which John describes here. The beasts of Daniel represent the power of the ruling nations of the world, the strength of man in his attempted independence from God. These powers considered themselves to be supreme and absolute in their day, but each has fallen in its turn.

This is the way it is with the thoughts and the dreams

of godless people, whether they lived in the twenty-first century B.C. or the twenty-first century A.D. They struggle to make their mark in the world, but regardless of the pinnacle of success which they may achieve, they all die and are soon forgotten. It is the same for individuals as it is for nations. They come, seek power and influence over others, and then they go. How much do you know about the Hittites or the Assyrians of old? Probably very little. Yet their nations once ruled the *known world!* Only God remains forever, and as the Psalmist writes, He laughs at the childish games of mankind (see Ps. 2:4).

This desire for earthly power and domination is what the beast from the sea represents. The sea, out of which this beast arises, is a sea of "peoples and multitudes **17:15** and nations and tongues" of the earth. Such godless people are futilely striving to write their claims to significance upon the tablets of this world's history, only to find that they have only been writing on water, leaving no lasting impression whatsoever. It does no good to ask, "Who is the sea-beast?" This creature represents a world-view, a way of life which seeks humanistically to exalt man to the point where he no longer needs God. This approach to life may be very fine and appropriate in the eyes of most people, but it is a lie. It seeks to give definition and meaning to life without reference to God.

Understanding the numbers of heads and horns on the beast (and on the dragon) is our next challenge. *Seven,* as said before, is a number usually attributed to God. It refers to the absolute and perfect. Here, in an unusual usage, the number seven is not applied to holy things but to the profane. The beast's seven heads indicate that it is absolutely evil and opposed to Jesus Christ's kingdom.

The number ten (and its multiples, one hundred and one thousand) is also used as a representation of wholeness or totality. The horn is an ancient symbol of earthly power. The heads and horns have this general meaning: The dragon and the beast, pictured with the seven heads and ten horns, represent the apparently absolute power of the antichrist powers of the world, as they muster together their strength to do spiritual battle with the ones who refuse to bow the knee to their satanic, humanistic authority.

The beast from the sea is given authority to act for **13:5** the forty-two month period between the first and second comings of Christ. Plainly, no one man has had authority during that whole period of time. However, the godless world-system which seeks to exalt man and to dethrone Christ has existed from the beginning of the age. It is humanistic, pagan worship which the sea-beast represents.

This beast receives an apparently "fatal wound" from **13:3** which it recovers. Here is another reference to one of the central themes of the Bible: the overthrow of the satanically-inspired, humanistic system of this world through the crucifixion and resurrection of Christ. Many throughout the age have chosen to ignore this victory **13:4** of Christ over the Evil One, and so the world-system has experienced resurrection from its death throes in the hearts of those who oppose Jesus and His church. Their new life is illusory, however, for Jesus Himself has promised us that He will return finally to crush Satan and his antichrist system under our feet (see Rom. 16:20). In the meantime, however, liberty is given **13:5,6** to the beast to continue to blaspheme God and to make war against Christ's church.

The history of the church is piled deep with examples of this warfare, from the days when Nero dipped Christians in pitch and used them as torches to light his parties, to the present time when our brothers and sisters are being tortured for Christ in Communist lands. Everyone who dwells on the earth, with the exception **13:8** of the elect whose names are written in the Book of Life, follows after this beast—even those who appear to be "nice guys." If one is not a follower of Jesus, he is a worshipper of the sea-beast, a participant in the kingdom of the Evil One. There is no neutral ground.

Man's False Religion: The Beast From the Earth

There is a second beast now introduced into the vision, the earth-beast. This creature does not have the hideous appearance of the first, but rather, it looks like a gentle, harmless lamb. Surely this is no beast to be feared like the first. What danger could arise from a lamb? **13:11**

Its innocuous appearance is precisely the threat of this lamb-like beast. Because it is so harmless in appearance, its deception can be all the more complete. For this beast does not speak with the voice of the true Lamb, nor does it honor Him; this lamb speaks with the voice of the dragon. What is the meaning of the beast's appearance?

That this beast has two horns like a lamb indicates that it is a religious symbol. Throughout the Book of Revelation the Lamb is the symbol of Christ, but this lamb is a counterfeit. Instead of leading people to God, it leads them astray. This lamb speaks gently and lovingly; but it uses the deceptive words of the dragon, Satan. In Revelation 16 this same character is called "the false prophet," again symbolizing his spiritually deceptive nature. **16:13**

All of this means that the earth-beast is a representation of the false religions of the world, which purport to tell men how they can know God but which actually lead them to fall under the deception of Satan. This does not mean that non-Christian religions are all outwardly and evidently evil. Far from it. But that is precisely the subtle nature of the earth-beast's deception. If your friends were asked if they would like to become Satan-worshippers, they would be horrified at the thought. The Devil knows this. He has a more in-

sidious plan. In the name of religion, morality, and the
love of humanity, your own friends as well as men and
women around the world throughout history have
believed they could be good enough to please God on
their own. But Jesus says, "No one comes to the Father
but through Me" (John 14:6).

Christ claims to be the only door to heaven, while the
false religions of the earth-beast deceive men into believing that they can make their own ways. The two religions could not be more opposed to one another: The
one is of Christ; the other is of Antichrist. This antichrist religion, in which all non-Christian religions have
a part, is represented by the beast out of the earth.

John tells us that this second beast exercises the **13:12**
authority of the first beast and that he makes all of the
earth worship it. This is precisely the case with the
man-centered religions of the world; all of them exalt
man into the rightful place of God. They bow down to **13:14**
the first beast as to an idol, the "image of the beast."
This type of man-worship began in the Garden of Eden
when the serpent promised Adam and Eve that they
would be like God if only they would assert their
autonomy and independence from God by rejecting His
way to eternal life (see Gen. 3:5).

Instead of glorifying the image of God in which he
was created, man has bowed down to the image of the
beast. We become like what we worship, either holy
like the true God or animalistic like the beast. The
serpent has never had to change this basic plan of
exalting man, because it has always worked so well, **13:15**
right down to today. The "I did it my way" philosophy
may sound very "in," but Jesus declares that those who
follow it will be "out" for all eternity.

The deception which is accomplished by the earth-
beast gives life to the already-defeated sea-beast. In
other words, the false religious systems of the world
perpetuate man's natural propensity to "do his own
thing" rather than God's. Many so-called ministers in
America today are telling their flocks to "be good" and

"try their best"—all well and good—but they leave out
the essential message of Christ crucified and risen. These
men are wolves in sleep's clothing. They are the ambassadors of the false prophet, and his deception is per-
petrated through them. Woe unto them and those who
follow after them, for their end is the lake of fire. Have
you recently examined the teaching you are receiving?

666: The Mark of the Beast

Now we come to a passage which has probably caused
as much speculation among Bible students as all other
passages combined. The last few verses of Revelation
13 speak of a mark which is found upon the right hands
or the foreheads of all of those who worship the beast.
The mark is said to consist of a number. "for the number is that of a man; and his number is six hundred and
sixty-six."

13:16–18

Who can resist guessing who 666 might be? What is
the mark, and how and when is it received? I have
heard various people teach that 666 is a symbol for
Caesar Nero, Martin Luther, Adolf Hitler, and Henry
Kissinger. Throughout church history there have been
scores of other candidates, none of whom have measured up (or down!) to expectations.

These guesses have come about through the use of an
ancient mystical practice called *gematria*. Gematria is
the study of the numerical value of people's names, a
value which is figured by ascribing a numerical value
to each letter in the alphabet (usually the Greek or
Hebrew alphabets) and then totaling the numbers of
all the letters in the name. One of the earliest examples of this practice pertains to the name of Caesar
Nero who seemed a "perfect 666" in the first century.
By transliterating the name Caesar Nero from Latin
into Hebrew (and then misspelling the name), a total of
666 can be reached. But the same sorts of things can be

said for the dozens of candidates for 666 which have been suggested down through history.

The very abundance of 666 nominees (often identified with Antichrist, although this connection is not made in the Bible), is in itself enough to call the faulty theory of gematria into question. In fact, I recently discovered that my own initials and last name, C. M. Colclasure, when transliterated into Hebrew and given numerical values, add up to 666 (no comments, please). The point is gematria offers no answer at all.

Hands and Foreheads

Let us try another avenue of solution, one which I believe to be the correct one. When we studied Revelation 7, we found that the seal of God is applied to the 7:3 foreheads of His people, the 144,000. Is that seal a physical mark or an invisible one? Should we expect that people in heaven, not to mention Christians still on the earth, will have some sort of physical tattoo upon their bodies so that God does not lose track of them? Of course not. This mark of God upon the forehead is a spiritual seal, signifying ownership through our union and identity with Christ.

We find an exact parallel in the Book of Exodus. There God speaks to the nation of Israel after He has led them out of the bondage of Egypt, and He admonishes them not to forget the redemption which He accomplished for them. In speaking of the commemoration of their deliverance, the Lord says to them, "It shall serve as a sign to you on your hand, and as a reminder on your forehead, that the law of the Lord may be in your mouth; for with a powerful hand the Lord brought you out of Egypt" (Ex. 13:9).

Here we have God speaking of a mark on the hand and upon the forehead. Was this a physical mark? Most assuredly not. God commanded his people not to mark or tattoo their bodies (see Lev. 19:28). No, this was a spiritual mark intended to be a reminder of God and His blessing, a sign that these redeemed ones were a people for his own possession. That it was to be upon their hand signified that all of their work, their labor, was to be for His glory. The sign on the forehead meant that all of their thoughts were to be honoring to Him and to bring about his praise. By thought, word, and deed the Israelites, carrying the mark of God, declared to the world they belonged to Him.

In Revelation, with the mark of the beast, we find the counterfeit of God's seal. Like the seal of God, the mark of the beast is an invisible, not a visible, sign. It signifies ownership. Those who bear the mark of the beast belong to him and live according to the rules of his world-system. Those of us without the mark of the beast, we who refuse to submit our minds to the programming of the world, will find it difficult to "buy and sell," to interact with the beast's ways of carrying on life day by day. No doubt you have experienced instances where your refusal to compromise with evil has cost you a promotion, a raise, or even your job. You refused to let your hands and mind participate in wrong. Nonetheless, we are sustained by God.

In the first verse of the next chapter, we who are **14:1** marked on our foreheads with the seal of God are contrasted with those who bear the mark of the beast. We are blessed; they are ultimately cursed.

666: The Number of Man

If then the mark of the beast is a spiritual rather **13:18** than a physical mark, what is the significance of the number 666?

In the original Greek text of Revelation 13:18, there is no article "a" before the word "man." (In fact, the Greek language does not even have such an article.) The verse really says that 666 is "the number of man." What else could that mean but humanity as a whole?

We have already learned that no one man has ruled

or lived for the whole church age. Further, mankind has been warring against God all along.

It is widely accepted that in the ancient world the number *six* represented mankind. Man was created on the sixth day. He is made a little lower than God; the number of perfection or deity is *seven*. Just as 777 could symbolize the perfect number of triune divinity, so a trinity of sixes, 666, would appropriately represent man's efforts to usurp the rightful position of God as the Sovereign of the universe. We are not dealing, then, with the number of *a* man. It is simultaneously the number of the beast and the number of rebellious mankind. For in fact, the spirit of the beast and the spirit of rebellious man are one and the same.

What this means for you is this: The real enemy of Christ and His church is not isolated to some "Future Führer" who will seek to rule the world. The real enemy is sinful mankind, controlled by Satan. Through the philosophy of secular humanism and a myriad of other man-made religions, the world is seeking to do away with Christ.

The good news is that Christ has already overcome this beast. Although it continues to rear its hideous head, as you believe you are an overcomer *par excellence* in Jesus Christ.

The Unholy Trinity

Another interesting observation may be made concerning the identities and relationships of the dragon, the sea-beast, and the earth-beast. These three characters in the Book of Revelation form a kind of "unholy trinity" which rivals the Father, Son, and Holy Spirit. This pseudotrinity can be clearly identified by comparing its activity with that of the Holy Trinity.

In the Holy Trinity, we usually think first of God the Father. He is the One who sent the Son into the world and who empowers Him to do His will. All of the authority of the Father is given to the Son, and the incarnate Son is the exact representation of the Father to men (see Matt. 28:18; Heb. 1:3). Because of the Son, men learn to worship rightly the Father (see John 4:23,24). The Son was dealt a mortal wound on the Cross, but He rose again to life, to carry on His ministry on our behalf (see 1 Cor. 15:3,4). The Holy Spirit proceeds from the Father and is sent by the Father and the Son to cause men to worship God rather than man (see John 14:16). It is the Holy Spirit who inspires us to good works, and who seals us into Christ, giving to us the mark of God (see Eph. 1:13).

Now notice the similarities between the counterfeit **13:1** trinity and the triune God. In Revelation 12 and 13, the dragon, parallel to the Father, initiates the coming of the sea-beast up out of the sea. The dragon gives to the sea-beast "his power and his throne and great authority." **13:2** The sea-beast, parallel to the Son, is the exact represen- **12:3** tation of the dragon, having the same number of heads and horns. Because of the activity of the sea-beast, "they **13:4** [the world] worshipped the dragon, because he gave his authority to the beast." Like Jesus, the beast was dealt **13:3** a mortal wound (through Christ's work on the Cross), but he has experienced a pseudo-resurrection and continues to infect the world with his poison. Just as the Holy Spirit causes some people to worship God, the earth-beast causes others "to worship the first beast, whose fatal **13:12** wound was healed." He brings about the performance of miraculous feats, "great signs" which deceive those who dwell **13:13** upon the earth into following the first beast. And the earth-beast causes the followers of the first beast to receive his mark as sign of their slavery to him. **13:16**

These counterfeit parallels are too precise to be accidental.

The 144,000: Another Look

These, then, are the four symbolic characters in Revelation 12 and 13: the woman, the dragon, the sea-beast, and the earth-beast. We now find the last three of the seven players on the stage of history as we look into chapter 14.

The first of these three is a great multitude we have **14:1** met before in chapter 7: the 144,000. We have already identified the 144,000 as the entire church of Christ throughout the ages, not a statistic but a symbol. The multitude is spoken of in terms which can apply only to the people of God, those who have been bought with the price of the death of Jesus. This means that what the Bible says about the 144,000 is true of you and me.

Notice first of all that the 144,000 are pictured as standing on Mount Zion, the holy mountain of God, with the Lamb Himself, Jesus Christ. Surely none but **14:3** the true church has ever occupied such a favored position. They are also, as we learned in chapter 7, sealed into Christ with the name of God on their foreheads. They are singing the "new song," the gospel of Christ, which can be learned only by those "who had been purchased from the earth." Obviously this multitude is joyously aware of God's special favor, the favor which is also ours in Jesus.

The next verses mention some rather unexpected traits **14:4** shared by the 144,000. First, they have not been defiled with women and are (literally) "male virgins." Second, they "follow the Lamb wherever He goes." Third, they have been "purchased from among men as first fruits to God and to the Lamb." Fourth, "no lie was found in **14:5** their mouth." Finally, we are told that they are "blameless." What should we make of this kind of language? Let's look at all five characteristics.

First of all, with regard to virginity, we are talking about spiritual purity. To say otherwise would demand that only male virgins who have never sinned be in the 144,000. There has been only One, Jesus Himself, who could be so qualified.

Throughout the Old Testament, Israel's unfaithfulness to Jehovah was represented in sexual terms. Israel was said to have committed adultery with the false gods of the nations around them (see Jer. 3:8). This adultery was, of course, a spiritual one. Christ, the Bridegroom of the church, expects His Bride to be pure, without spot or blemish, when He returns to take her to the marriage supper of the Lamb (see Eph. 5:27). Thus He is pleased with those who have turned from spiritual adultery. The "women" who threaten to defile the 144,000 represent false gods and disobedient living, the double stumblingblocks which trip up many who claim the name of Jesus. If you are truly Christ's, though you continue to sin, you will not marry yourself to false teaching nor unbiblical life-styles. You will seek to remain pure and obedient to your Savior and Lord.

Second, we follow the Lamb wherever He goes. We do **14:4** not take Him as our Savior, then do as we please. Jesus is *both* Lord and Savior. His two titles are indivisible. You do not make Jesus Lord—He already *is* the Lord. Regardless of whether men acknowledge it or not, God has made Him both Lord and Christ (see Acts 2:36). Those of us who belong to the 144,000 must learn this lesson well.

Third, the 144,000 have also been purchased from among men by the blood of Jesus, a point we have already emphasized.

Fourth, they speak no lies, only the truth. The truth which they speak is the gospel of Jesus, who said, "I **14:5** am...the truth" (John 14:6).

Fifth, they are blameless. All of us are sinners, but the blame, the guilt for sin has been removed from us if we are numbered in the 144,000. The penalty of sin, eternal death, has already been paid for us by Another, and transferred to His account. We have no blame, for there is "no condemnation for those who are in Christ Jesus" (Rom. 8:1).

All of these five blessings belong to you as you belong to Jesus. God desires to comfort you as His child with the knowledge that He takes special note of you, and that He will see you through your assorted trials and temptations.

The Three Angels

The sixth character in the series of seven personages **14:6–** is made up of a trio of beings, three angels. Each of **12** these angels has a special message to proclaim to the peoples of the earth, and their three proclamations are the immediate precursors to the return of the Son of Man, Jesus Christ, at the end of the world. These angelic voices, then, serve as final warnings to those who continue to be the enemies of God and of His Christ. While other characters in chapters 12 and 13 were all representative of the circumstances which have existed in the world since the first century, these three angels and their cries bring to pass the end of time.

But even though these messages have special import as final warnings, their meanings are nevertheless crucial for us today. Through the warnings of these three angels, two truths are seen. The first is that God's patience with unrepentant men and women is not without limits. He will forewarn those who are the objects of His wrath, but if they continue to refuse His mercy, they will taste of His justice. Second, those of us who believe are assured that God's justice and righteousness will win out. We shall be counted as overcomers with Him.

The first of the three angels proclaims that "the hour **14:7** of His judgment has come." Therefore all those on the earth should be careful to "fear God, and give Him glory...and worship Him...." Those who do not, have the wrath of God abiding upon them. When the Day of Judgment is upon them they will find that he who does not honor the Son does not honor the Father who sent Him (see John 5:23).

Many people I meet today say that they believe in God, but they do not want anything to do with Jesus. The Scripture says there is only one God, and that God is the Father of our Lord Jesus Christ. If the God one worships is not the Father of Jesus Christ, then it is the wrong god. Such a god is no more than an idol.

The second angel proclaims the fall of the great city **14:8** of this world, "Babylon the great." Ancient Babylon was the place in the Old Testament (known in its early years as Babel) where men first joined together in their rebellion against God (see Gen. 11:1–9). They sought to throw off His restraints upon them by building a tower to reach God through their own efforts. As the city of Babylon grew it became associated with all forms of immorality, occultism, and idolatry. Thus "Babylon" is a fit name for the whole world of the present age, which despite its various political and cultural divisions is united in this one thing: opposition to Jesus Christ and His people.

This second angel announces that the godless system of Babylon has been defeated and thrown down. Just as the sea-beast was defeated through the Cross and yet continues to live on for a time in the world, so the godless Babylon, the kingdom of the beast, has enjoyed a fleeting prosperity in this present evil age. But as the day of God's judgment draws nigh, the crumbling of Babylon becomes evident. This is both a warning to the citizens of Babylon and a joy to those who belong to the heavenly city of Christ waiting the full inauguration of the New Jerusalem of God.

The final angel cries out concerning those who have **14:9** received the mark of the beast on their hands or foreheads. Although they may have been able to buy and sell in this world, in the eternal age to come they will experience eternal, spiritual poverty and the unending torment of the anger of God.

This passage presents an arresting image. We are told that those who have followed after the beast "will be tormented with fire and brimstone in the presence **14:10** of the holy angels and in the presence of the Lamb." So many people, even Christians, have accepted the caricature of Christ which depicts Him as "gentle Jesus, meek and mild"—a poor little Jesus who can't do a thing unless men let Him, and who wouldn't harm a fly.

While it is certainly true that the compassion and mercy of Jesus Christ toward repentant sinners is infinite, the Bible tells us that His anger with those who sin with impunity is unending. Those who have mocked the One they have misinterpreted as a weakling Jesus will find that because of His holy might, they will have no rest, day or night. The messages of the three angels are the last warnings to a rebellious and Christ-hating world. Perhaps their voices are already sounding.

The Coming of the Son of Man

The last and greatest of the seven characters revealed **14:14** in Revelation 12–14 is "one like a son of man, having a golden crown on His head, and a sharp sickle in His hand." This seventh personage in the vision is Jesus Christ Himself, returning at the end of the world to reap the harvest of the earth and to bring about its final judgment. The three angels have proclaimed that "the hour of His judgment has come." Now, that judgment is revealed.

The use of harvest imagery in reference to the judgment is common throughout the Bible (see Matt. 13:24–30, 36–40). Perhaps the best known is the parable of the wheat and the tares, in which good and evil are allowed to grow together in the field of the world until the harvest day. "Allow both to grow together until the harvest," Jesus says, "and in the time of the harvest I will say to the reapers, 'First gather up the tares and bind them in bundles to burn them up; but gather the wheat into my barn' " (v.30).

The picture in Revelation 14 is the same. The Son of Man initiates this day of harvesting the earth, and the angels carry it out. The unbelievers of the world are pictured as grapes being thrown into a wine press and crushed together. But instead of the juice of the grape it is the blood of men which pours forth. God does not mince words, does He? The judgment is so severe that the blood runs deep for a distance of 1,600 *stadia* (according to the Greek). (Sixteen hundred *stadia* would measure over 181 miles!)

14:15– 20

Once again we find a number in the Revelation which is not statistical but spiritual. We have discovered earlier that *four* is often used as a numerical value signifying all of creation. The value of 1,600 may be broken down into the factors $4 \times 4 \times 100$. In other words, we are being taught in this vision that the extent of judgment of the Last Day will reach into all of creation, and that those who have not had Jesus' blood shed on their behalf will have their own spilt because of their sins.

Revelation 14, then, like chapters 6 and 11, ends with a scene depicting the return of Christ at the end of the world. These accounts can be terrifying, but nevertheless they offer hope—hope of repentance for the rebel and hope of eternal victory for the faithful.

7. The Wrath of God

From time to time things unplanned and disappointing happen in each of our lives. There is often very little we can do to rectify the resulting circumstances. We all need to learn, as I'm sure you've discovered, to roll with life's punches.

This is the meaning of the old saying, "There's no use in crying over spilt milk," and it is true, so far as it goes. We should not waste time bemoaning past mistakes, particularly those as minor as "spilt milk." Once certain things are done, they cannot be undone.

But there is something which can indeed be done to cancel out sin against God: We must confess our sins, turn from them, and be reconciled to God and the people our sin has harmed. Those who are willing to confess and turn from their sins will also see the need for someone to bear away the penalty of sin for them, and this is what the Lord Jesus Christ does for us who trust in Him.

As we watch the Revelation's seven bowls full of the wrath of God being emptied upon the unbelieving world, those who are the enemies of Christ begin to understand that both their own rebellion and the justice of God poured out upon them are infinitely more consequential than spilt milk.

The Bowls Full of God's Wrath

As we examine these seven bowls "full of the wrath of God" which are poured out upon the rebellious and unbelieving world, we will see a great similarity be-

131

tween the effects of these "bowl judgments" and those which arose from the blowing of the seven trumpets.

You will remember we saw in the trumpet judgments a close association between the plagues they brought about and those which were unleashed upon ancient Egypt in the days of Moses.

In Revelation 16, we see the same principle of interpretation being used but with some significant differences in emphases. Whereas the trumpet's plagues were described as affecting "one third" of the creation, no such limitation is found in the bowls. Their effects are universal in scope. And whereas the trumpets spared men their direct intensity, the bowls' afflictions immediately touch unrepentant men with the displeasure of God and the accompanying torments.

Does this mean that the judgments of the bowls are therefore to be uniquely felt sometime in the unforeseen future, having no effect in the present world? Or that the judgments of the bowls come *after* those of the trumpets? No, not at all.

We must remember God deals with each person and with each generation of men individually. While the world is spoken of in the Scriptures as if it were a single entity, it is made up of millions of individual viewpoints, attitudes, and lives. Because this is true, God applies His discipline (and His punishment) to people as individuals, as well as in groups. It is entirely possible (and daily life often shows it to be true) that God would apply the seemingly "less severe" judgments of the trumpets as a warning to one individual or group. Those to whom the bowls' severe judgments are applied are those who have persisted in their rebellion even after many warnings.

The First Bowl: Malignant Sores and Sin

Let's find out what the pouring out of these wrathful bowls means. As this vision opens, the voice of the Lord   **16:1** is heard coming out from the temple, declaring the time has come for the extreme punishment of the bowls to be meted out. The fact that this is God's voice reminds us again that He is in control, even in the midst of what appear to be mindless tragedies. And since it is God Himself who calls for the bowls to be poured out, He can be trusted to administer precisely what is needed to bring about true justice and His own glory—as well as the ultimate welfare of those who love Him.

The first bowl causes a malignant sore to afflict those **16:2** who bear the mark of the beast. We have already seen that all of those who have rejected the Lord Jesus Christ bear that mark of the Evil One's ownership. From this we know that this plague (as well as those of the other bowls) does not affect the church, but rather its enemies.

This first bowl's plague is reminiscent of the plague of boils which God brought upon Pharaoh and his people by the hand of Moses (see Ex. 9:9–11). In spite of this affliction, which fell upon all Egyptians from the royal court to the lowliest slave, Pharaoh's heart remained hardened, and he refused to obey the word of Jehovah.

Look around you. Don't you see the same thing happening in the world today? Let's face it: God afflicts men and women just as in days of old. Why did God plague Egypt? So that the hardened Egyptians would repent and His people Israel could see His power. Why does He plague people today? For the same reasons: that unbelievers might turn to Him and that His people might have the opportunity to see their faith tested in the crucible of affliction.

But some people are so hardened that if they are to have any opportunity at all to turn to the living Lord, God has to first "get their attention" through affliction. These are the ones upon whom the bowls are poured out. It is not the greatest compliment to God that we choose Him only as a last resort, but even when we come to Him by the process of elimination(when we find out that nothing else works), Jesus is still waiting to receive us. Amazing love! And just as amazing is His severity with those who refuse to obey Him.

The Second Bowl: Death on the Seas

Like the first trumpet, the first bowl affects things on the earth (in this case, men and women). And like the second trumpet, the second bowl brings about judg- **16:3** ment upon the seas, turning them to "blood." Again we see the reference to the judgments of Egypt, where the Lord caused the waters of that land to become useless when He turned the Nile to blood (see Ex. 7:20,21). But once more we note a difference in the midst of similarity. Whereas the second trumpet causes one third **8:8** of the sea to become blood, the second bowl causes "every living thing in the sea" to die.

Are we to understand that the H_2O of the sea waters will someday, somehow, change its chemical composition so that it is transformed into the stuff that courses through our veins? No. The point here is that the seas, representing that which had been understood for centuries to be the source of man's life, provision, and commerce, will at the command of God be turned into death, dead man's blood. Every edifice upon which men hang their hopes for prosperity can be instantly razed by the finger of God. He alone is eternally dependable, and it is only when we rest in Him that we can be truly secure.

How fragile are the lives of those who profess themselves to be almighty! Because they refuse to come before God in worship, they must come before Him in judgment. In the end, *every* knee shall bow, but only a few willingly.

The Third Bowl: Foul Waters

The plague accompanying the third bowl is also an **16:4**
intensified version of its counterpart in the trumpet
judgments. Here, as with the third trumpet, the rivers **8:10,11**
and springs (fresh waters) are touched with judgment,
turning as the sea did to blood. The meaning of this
bowl complements that of the second, and it adds the
emphasis of the universality of God's justice. The whole
earth, the land, the seas, and the land waters are un-
able to escape the pervasive hand of God's righteous
wrath against man's rebellion.

An interesting commentary is added by "the angel of **16:5**
the waters," declaring the fitting nature of God's retri-
bution upon the enemies of Christ and His people. "They
poured out the blood of saints and prophets, and Thou
hast given them blood to drink. They deserve it."   **16:6**

A response to this comment comes from a voice at the
altar (which reminds us of the martyred saints we saw
represented there in the opening of the fifth seal): " 'Yes, **16:7**
O Lord God, the Almighty, true and righteous are Thy
judgments.' "

As fallen and sinful human beings, our concepts of
fairness and justice are warped. We are generally either too severe or too lenient in our judgments, too
swift to anger or too slow to respond to sin. But these
verses remind us this is not so with God. His justice is
perfect. Because the world has spilled the blood of God's
people, God gives them the blood they so eagerly
sought—except this time it is their own demise rather
than the death which they sought to bring upon the
church.

We may rest assured that the injustices which we see
continuing day by day in this world someday will be set
aright. I get so frustrated watching helplessly as evil
wins out and good goes unrewarded. But it will not be
so at the end. That knowledge should give those of us

who know and love Jesus both patience and compassion: Patience because we know that God will do what is best at exactly the right time, and compassion even for our enemies, for we know that unless they repent and turn to Christ, an unspeakably terrifying eternity awaits them.

Instead of seeking revenge, therefore, we should desire to bring the enemies of God into the hearing of the gospel, that they might become His sons and receive His mercy, just as we have. When we refuse to fight someone, we put him out of business as an enemy. Therefore, do not repay evil for evil, but leave room for the justice of God (see Rom. 12:17,19). He alone knows what the word really means.

The Fourth Bowl: The Fire of the Sun

With the pouring out of the fourth bowl the parallel to the trumpet cycle continues. Just as the fourth trumpet sounded out affliction for the heavens, so the emptying of the fourth bowl does the same, only intensified. The fourth trumpet affected one third of the heavens, but no such limitation is mentioned with this bowl. **16:8 8:12**

Like the first bowl, this fourth afflicts men personally: They are "scorched with fierce heat." The response of the plagued men is important to see here. Instead of being brought to repentance as a result of God's warnings to them, these men "blasphemed the name of God who has the power over these plagues; and they did not repent, so as to give Him glory." **16:9**

It is perhaps at this point that the people of Christ and the people of the world are most diametrically different. How do you respond in the face of suffering? We who trust in the sovereign love of Jesus Christ know one thing even when all else remains hidden: Jesus loves and cares for His sheep. Because I know that, I can receive willingly—even thankfully—tribulations and difficulties, insults and slanders, life and death.

All that happens to you is in His watchful care. He did not have His head turned when your loved one was struck down. He was not napping when your "friends" turned away from you because you became a Christian. And He is mindful of you even now, with all of your hurts and sorrows and sins. If you are His, He will never leave you nor forsake you (see Heb. 13:5). For you, suffering has a divine purpose, and your realization of that truth should enable you to endure whatever befalls you with patience and thanksgiving (see 1 Pet. 2:20,21).

But what of the unbeliever? He is the one we find under the torment of the fourth bowl. He curses God, and thereby drives himself farther from the only One who can possibly offer him hope. He refuses the call to repentance, and thus seals himself off from the saving hand of God. He sees no purpose in his suffering; it is meaningless to him.

It is difficult enough to endure the pains of this world when we know that a sovereign God directs them, but if one believes that there is no reason or ultimate good to be derived from difficulties, afflictions become unbearable. The unbeliever refuses to hear the voice of the One who says, "Cast all of your burdens upon Me" (see 1 Pet. 5:7), and so he has to carry them all himself. This is the meaning of nonfaith, and its invariable results are curses and blasphemies.

The sun is said to be the particular target of the fourth bowl's outpouring. This completes the universal effects of the wrath of God against those who refuse to bow the knee. The earth, the sea, the rivers, and the heavens are all likewise cursed by the response of God to mankind's sin. Where can one go to escape the justice of God? There is no place to hide. Like God Himself, His restitution is omnipresent. The only way to flee from God is to flee to Him. This is the truth which comforts the church in this evil age. We have escaped His anger by taking refuge in His mercy.

The Fifth Bowl:
The Beast's Kingdom Darkened

When the fifth angel pours out his bowl upon the **16:10** earth, the very throne of the beast is affected, "and his kingdom became darkened." Those who are citizens in that kingdom of rebellion receive the just due of their verbal blasphemy: Men gnaw their tongues because of the pain they suffer.

This bowl's effects show us the great irony which accompanies following after the antichrist world-system of the beast. Men refuse to follow Christ because His is the narrow road, the difficult way. The world promises a shortcut to happiness and fulfillment. "You can do it without Christ," the beast cries out, and the children of the world hear and follow. "Come, be free from the chains of God and religion, be liberated, escape the bondage of commandment and law."

But too late it is discovered that what was purported to be freedom has turned out to be slavery, and that which was called light has become darkness. Happiness has turned to mourning, and fulfillment to emptiness.

The fifth bowl tells this story, for by it the kingdom of darkness is finally revealed to be what it actually is. Even though Satan can appear as an angel of light (see 2 Cor. 11:14), in the end his identity as the prince of darkness will be understood by all, most terribly by those who chose to follow him and serve in his kingdom.

Even at that point, when the darkness of the beast's world-system is revealed, men refuse God's offer of forgiveness. "They did not repent of their deeds," and "they blasphemed the God of heaven because of their pains." **16:11**

The Sixth Bowl:
Preparation for the Final War

With the blowing of the sixth trumpet a tremendous **9:13–19**
demonic influence is released upon the unbelieving world,
represented by the fantastic horsemen and their steeds
in Revelation 9. They are described as being bound at
the Euphrates River which, you will recall, was considered to be the ancient boundary of the nation Israel.
From the New Testament perspective, the new Israel is
the church. Thus we understand that, according to the
trumpet vision, God brings about attacks, not upon the
church, but upon the unbelieving world. Unbelievers
are receiving a deluding influence so as to believe what
is false (see 2 Thess. 2:11), while we who are Christ's
are led into the truth.

We are reminded of that same principle here in the **16:12**
outpouring of the sixth bowl. Again the Euphrates is
mentioned, and the demonic armies are described in no
uncertain terms. The "kings from the east" as well as "the **16:13**
kings of the whole world" are empowered by "spirits"
which proceed out of the mouth of the dragon (Satan),
the beast (the evil world-system), and the false prophet
(earlier called the "beast from the earth," the world's
false religious systems). We are told specifically that
the empowering forces behind these kings and their
armies are spirits of demons, and that these demons
perform deceptive signs to mislead the whole world.

As the result of all this, the whole world (represented
by its kings) gathers itself for final battle against the
people of God. We have seen this battle described before **11:7,8**
in the description of the two witnesses in the great city **19:19**
in Revelation 11, and we will find it described again in **20:8,9**
Revelation 19 and 20.

Throughout this entire age there has been a battle
raging between the armies of two kingdoms, the kingdom of the beast and the kingdom of Christ. It has

often appeared that the kingdom of the beast was winning the fray, and it may seem so right up until the end. But at the climax of history, just when it seems that the church can stand no more, the Lord Himself will come to claim victory for us and put an end to the kingdom of darkness forever. This final battle is "the war of the great day of God, the Almighty," and it culminates with the coming of Christ and the end of the world. **16:14**

Thus, in the midst of a rather frightening vision of the spiritual armies of evil which do battle with the church, Jesus speaks words of comfort to us: "Behold, I am coming like a thief. Blessed is the one who stays awake and keeps his garments, lest he walk about naked and men see his shame." Just before we learn of the final curse upon the kingdom of the beast, a blessing is pronounced by Christ Himself upon all who remain faithful to Him until the end. In the midst of a perverse and evil generation we could lose heart. So remember: *The Lamb wins!* **16:15**

This brings us to the mention of the place of the battle between the church and the world: Har-Magedon. This is a reference to the famous "Battle of Armageddon," a phrase often associated with the end of the world. **16:16**

There are a number of truths which must be understood before we can correctly discern the meaning of the battle. First, this is the final battle in a great spiritual war which has been waged from the beginning of the age until now.

Second, it is a battle which is fought between the forces of the Evil One and the armies of Christ. Thus, its combatants are the world and the church, set against one another for a fight to the death. It is therefore plain that this is not a military battle fought between political nations of the earth with the weapons, nuclear or otherwise, of the world. This is the conflict of darkness *vs.* light; we must therefore, as Paul reminds us, be prepared to fight it with spiritual weapons, not fleshly ones (see Eph. 6:12,13).

Third, though this conflict has been waged since the

beginning of the age, it increases in intensity as the
Last Day nears. Fourth, its outcome is certain: Jesus
Christ, through His mighty work on the Cross and His
return in glory, will be finally and absolutely victorious
over the armies of the beast. The church will overcome.

If this is all true, why the oft-heard reference to the
mountain of Megiddo, a real geographical location?
Doesn't that imply that there will be a physical battle
on a physical battlefield near the hill of Megiddo in
Israel? At first glance, it might seem so. But despite
initial appearances, that is not the case.

In the days of ancient Israel, Megiddo was a very
important city. It lay at the junction of the most important trade routes of the Middle East. Whoever controlled
Megiddo controlled much of the commerce of the Middle East. Whoever controlled Megiddo also controlled
much of the military strength of the day. Pharaoh Necho
of ancient Egypt wrote, "He who takes Megiddo has
taken a thousand cities."

Because of the city's crucial position, any battle for
control of Megiddo was a key conflict, often the decisive
battle of the war. Thus, the term "battle of Armageddon"
came to mean the decisive battle which determines the
ultimate victor in a conflict.

In the Revelation, John uses the phrase in just this
way. The battle of Armageddon is not a political battle
at a geographical location. Instead it signifies the decisive battle in the age-old conflict between Christ and
Satan, between the Lamb and the dragon, between the
church and the world.

You are a soldier in one of the armies fighting in that
warfare. If you belong to Christ, then you have entered
the conflict whether you like it or not. The issue in your
life is not "Should I enlist in Jesus' army?" You've already been drafted! The question which does remain is
this: Will you be a loyal, hard-fighting soldier, or will
you be found A.W.O.L.? Jesus gave His life for you. Can
you do less for Him?

The sixth bowl then, like the sixth trumpet, brings us to the very brink of the end of the age. The final consummation is described in the pouring out of the final bowl.

The Seventh Bowl: The End of the World

That judgment which was begun at the command of the voice of God coming out of the temple in heaven is now completed with the final pronouncement of that same voice: "It is done." Just as God by a word called the world into existence, so with a word He brings it to an end. This is the meaning of the seventh bowl. **16:17**

We have already learned that flashes of lightning, thunder, and a great earthquake are used in the Revelation as accompaniments to the end of the world. It is significant that these phenomena are also used elsewhere to portend the presence of the all-holy God (see Ex. 19:16). Thus the end of the world and the presence of Christ are coupled in these images, as they shall be joined in reality at the return of Christ the Lord at the end of the age. **16:18 6:12 11:19**

We read that the great city is split asunder by the great earthquake of the Last Day. This city is the same one described as falling in the blowing of the seventh trumpet, the city which sought the death of the witnesses and which crucified Christ. As this wicked world-system falls, all individually rebellious nations fall with it. "Babylon the great," another name for that beastly reign, is destroyed by Christ at His coming. Babylon imbibes deeply of the wine of the wrath of God, and as we will see in the next vision, she is forced to drink it mixed at twice its strength on that Day of Judgment. **16:19 11:8 18:6**

We learned from the opening of the sixth seal that at the end of the world "every mountain and island were moved out of their places." We find this peculiar fact recorded here as well. **16:20 6:14**

As the world draws to a close, as the forces of nature **16:21** rage against man (who originally brought about the fall of the creation through his sin), people are still unrepentant, blaspheming God with the last breaths they breathe. Such men will endure a terrible judgment in hell, but who can say that it is not deserved? The wonderfully amazing thing is this: I, too, deserve that terrible judgment, but Christ has already gone through it for me. Since He has suffered it in my place, there is no further debt for me to pay. As the song says, "Jesus paid it all, all to Him I owe."

The grace of God is free. But it is not cheap. It cost the Father the life of His Son. Can we receive this grace with anything less than a full commitment of our own lives to Him?

The Bowls Reviewed

It is plain that the pouring out of these bowls of the wrath of God is much, much more than spilt milk. We must not take the warnings of God's wrath against sin lightly.

God demonstrates to us again in this vision what He has affirmed in the previous ones: During this age there will be trouble in the world. Men and creation will both be affected by these troubles. Those who refuse to turn to Christ in response to God's warnings will be punished in the end, for as rebels they have been the instigators and the perpetrators of the world's evils.

In all of this, the message for you, a child of God, is that the Father is sovereign and omnipotent. Your prayers will be answered; He is in control. When your prayers seem not to be answered, He is still in control. Your God is sovereign even when you don't recognize it, but the secret of making your life joyous is in learning to see His mighty hand behind every happening. When you learn that, you can be "anxious for nothing" (Phil. 4:6). Then, and only then, will you truly understand the message of the Revelation.

8. Hardhearted Harlot

It is one of the peculiarities of our time that we have become a people who have trouble speaking plainly. Very rarely these days can one be found who "will call a spade a spade." There is a song which goes, "Honesty, such a lonely word—everyone is so untrue."

This tendency among us shows up in our universal use of euphemisms. No one commits the sins of *adultery* or *fornication* anymore. People just have "affairs." Nobody these days is an *idolater*. Folks merely have "wrong priorities." And you'll not meet a *covetous* person today, either; just someone who's "looking out for number one." Homosexuals are "gay," men and women rebelling against God and society are "liberated," marriages without commitment are called "open."

And have you noticed how TV and movies depict the prostitute? She (or he) is not seen as a sinner in need of repentance and forgiveness. Instead the streetwalker is a mistreated woman who has been sinned against by society. The man who sells his soul for his business is simply "by nature" a workaholic who knows how to get ahead. Their problems are not their fault. They are really not responsible. What a far cry from the biblical revelation. While the Bible always offers hope for the prostitute—or to any sinner who will repent—Scripture is never soft in its attitude toward sin.

As we turn to the 17th chapter of the Revelation, we meet there a gaudy, seductive prostitute. But there are no fancy, nice-sounding words used in her description. This woman is plainly and simply a *whore*—a devious, destructive, hardhearted harlot.

In some ways, this vision of the harlot is the most difficult of all the scenes of the Revelation to decipher. Its general meaning, taken in the context of the book as a whole, seems very plain. But when we try to get down to specifics, the study gets a bit tougher. Perhaps in the generality of the meaning of this vision lies its greatest value: Every generation of Christians since the time of John has been able to identify the presence of the harlot in its own time. She represents the seductive attractiveness of the beast's world-system. But before we get ahead of ourselves, let's examine the first few verses of the chapter.

The Unhappy Hooker: Babylon, the Great

This vision opens as one of the angels John had seen **17:1** in the previous scene introduces him to the cast of characters who enact what follows. The angel describes "the great harlot" who has corrupted "the kings of the earth" and "those who dwell on the earth." The re- **17:2** sult of her influence has been "immorality," which we understand in this visionary context to mean all the sorts of rebelliousness of man against his Creator.

After this verbal prologue, the angel transports John "into a wilderness" where the harlot is seen riding on **17:3** the back of a scarlet beast, which has seven heads and ten horns. She is clothed opulently in expensive garments, she wears the richest of gems, and she bears a **17:4** golden chalice. Quite a striking figure. She has probably made herself up to be very attractive in a perverse sort of way.

But as John looks closer, he sees that the ornate cup she holds is filled with filth, and her name is visible upon her forehead: "BABYLON THE GREAT, THE MOTHER OF HARLOTS AND OF THE ABOMINATIONS OF THE EARTH." The woman is reeling in her drunk- **17:5** enness, for she has drunk deeply of "the blood of the saints, and with the blood of the witnesses of Jesus."

This harlot represents the seductive and deadly at-   **17:6**
tractiveness of the beast's kingdom. But what are we to
learn from this nightmarish scene?

The Beast Revisited

The angel's reply to John's wonderment gives us some   **17:7**
hope that he will help us to understand the meaning of
this vision: "I shall tell you the mystery of the woman
and of the beast that carries her...." But that hope of a
simple solution is dashed with the angel's explanation,
which is most mysterious. Is there any way to get to the
underlying meaning of all of this?

I think there is, if we are careful to pay attention to
the relationship of this scene with previous ones we
have seen.

First comes the identification of the beast itself: It   **17:8**
"was and is not, and is about to come up out of the
abyss and to go to destruction." We have met this beast
before, haven't we? This is the seven-headed, ten-horned
beast of chapter 12. We learned there that this monster
symbolizes the godless world-system, typified by desires
for living life without reference to Jesus Christ and for
the deification of man. These things, as we have seen in
earlier chapters, are characteristic not only of the world
today. They have been typical of the unbelievers' world
views from the beginning of the age. The beast of this
vision is the same beast we encountered before. Here
we see another aspect of its evil.

But first, what does it mean that this beast "was and
is not, and is about to come up out of the abyss?" This
trilogy of time refers to the worldwide deception of Satan,
his binding (which took place at the Cross of Jesus),
and his release near the end of the age.

Satan's universal deception continued unimpeded before the coming of Christ. But since the incarnation,
crucifixion and resurrection of Jesus Christ, Satan's
blinding of the Gentiles has been greatly diminished.

Jesus is, after all, the "light which... enlightens every man" (John 1:9). Through the power of His gospel, Jesus Christ has bound Satan from deceiving the nations. The Scripture predicts, however, that near the end of the age, Satan's power will be restored for a short time.

Back in chapter 11, we saw a reference to "the beast **11:7** that comes up out of the abyss" immediately before the return of Christ. When we come to chapter 20, we will **20:1–3** again see a reference to both the binding of the Evil One at the Cross and his subsequent release just before the final judgment.

Each of these references to the binding and releasing of Satan, although they are found in different chapters of the Revelation, refer to the same events. They are recounted in the several parallel accounts of the history of the age which make up the Revelation.

What all this means is this: Before Christ's birth, death, and resurrection, Satan was free to roam about the earth, deceiving the nations and blinding them from beholding the light of God's truth. In terms of his sway over the world, the beast "was." But at the Cross this deceptive power was greatly limited. Authority over the earth was shifted to Christ, and so in this present age, though the Evil One still rules in the hearts of rebellious men, his totality of power "is not" as it was. Yet to come will be a time immediately preceding the end of the world when Satan is once again allowed to practice his worldwide deception unimpeded. The final rebellion brought about at that time will foment the climax of spiritual conflict and lead to the end of the world.

In other words, the Devil's power has been limited since the time of the Cross, for there Christ bound Satan from deceiving the nations. How? The church has been planted all over the earth. In the old covenant, God's presence was uniquely with one nation, Israel. In the new covenant, all nations of the earth are blessed with the presence of Christ in His church. Thus the beast, activated by the power of the Evil One, can be said to have been powerful *before* the Cross, restricted greatly in its power *since* the Cross (until just before the end of the age), and *powerful again* in the final days of the world. He "was, and is not, and is about to come...."

World conditions today point to the possibility he has been released even now. The gospel is being silenced in more and more areas of the world. Dangers appear to be growing worse and worse in nearly every sphere of world, national, and personal concern. But we who belong to Jesus need not fear, even if it becomes still more apparent that we may be in those last moments of history. Because our names have been "written from the foun- **13:8** dation of the world in the book of life of the Lamb," we are secure in our relationship with the great Overcomer, Jesus. On the other hand, the beast, we are assured, will "go to destruction," being cast into the lake of fire forever. (Compare this to the true God, as discussed in **1:8** chapter 1, "who is and who was and who is to come.")

The Mystery of the Seven Heads

In the next verses, the mystery of the seven heads of **17:9** the beast is revealed. We are told first that "the seven heads are seven mountains on which the woman sits." To any first-century reader, this would have been recognized as a reference to the city of Rome. Even today, Rome is known as the "City of Seven Hills."

This reference to the seven mountains is meant to direct our attention to the Rome of John's day. First-century Rome was the center of a great empire, one which covered most of the then-known world. Rome had contributed much to the culture and advancement of the human race, but that city is used here as a symbol of evil, particularly the kind of wickedness which seeks to destroy the people of God.

Although Rome was tolerant of the Christian sect for a few years, by the time of John's death a number of violent, Roman-inspired persecutions against the church had occurred. Thus, in a larger sense, this reference to Rome can be understood to include *all* of the world's opposition to the people of God. In the early centuries that persecution came chiefly from the Roman Empire, but later on other powers took over afflicting the church where Rome left off.

Seven Heads, Seven Kings

The seven heads are also seven "kings," the angel **17:10** interprets. Not only do the seven heads represent Rome in relation to the church, but they also represent seven kings or kingdoms. Some historians have tried to fit the various emperors of Rome into this sevenfold scheme. But I believe that a better understanding sees these seven kings not as individual men, but as world empires.

"Five have fallen, one is, the other has not yet come," we are told of these kingdoms. Before the advent of the Roman Empire, there had been five major world kingdoms: the Old Babylonian, the Assyrian, the New Babylonian, the Mede-Persian, and the Greco-Macedonian Empires. By the time of Rome, those five had fallen.

Rome itself is the kingdom that "is" at the time of John's writing. That leaves us with the task of determining the identity of the other king who had not yet arisen by John's day.

Since the time of the fall of the Roman Empire there has been no single nation which has established supremacy on the earth. Empires have come and gone, but none have rivaled the expanse of power and absolute authority of those of the ancient world. It is not within the realm of political or military empires that we must look for this seventh kingdom. This final kingdom is not limited to geographical or political boundaries, for it transcends all earthly lines of demarcation. This seventh kingdom is in the world today: It *is* the world today! How do we know that?

The one characteristic shared by the first five king-doms which existed before Rome (which was also ev-ident in the Roman Empire) was univocal opposition to the people of God. Representatives from each of those six empires attacked and persecuted the believers in Jehovah. Now, since the fall of Rome, a new kingdom has come into existence, and this one "must remain a little while." This kingdom is the entire unbelieving world, which, like the preceding kingdoms, has become united in one thing: a common hatred for the church of Jesus Christ.

The kingdom of the beast, empowered by the Evil **17:11** One himself, is (literally) "of the seven." It belongs to them and they to it. All of those previous kingdoms were merely different manifestations of the beast's rule, a rule which has continued through the ages and which has now spread to cover the earth. His kingdom encom-passes and empowers all of the others.

What this means, of course, is that as a believer in Christ you must not become a friend of the world, for it is opposed to Christ. "If anyone loves the world, the love of the Father is not in him" (1 John 2:15). You should not be surprised that the world does not love you, for the Lord Jesus has warned us, "I chose you out of the world, therefore the world hates you" (John 15:19).

As followers of Jesus, we must arm ourselves for spiritual battle. We are at war! We must not, through compromise, be guilty of aiding and abetting the ene-my. Know this: There is no neutral area, no demilitarized zone. Every heart is a battlefield, and no person can remain uninvolved or unaffected. As Jesus said, "He who is not with Me is against Me" (Matt. 12:30).

Ten Horns, Ten Kings

The ten horns which protrude from the beast's seven **17:12,** heads "receive authority as kings with the beast for **13** one hour. These have one purpose and they give their power and authority to the beast." Who are these ten kings, and what do they represent?

We have seen earlier how the number ten and its multiples are used in the Revelation to signify wholeness or completeness. The meaning here is no different. These ten kings stand for all of the smaller and less significant kingdoms which have arisen during this age. They are many, but their authority and power has lasted for only a brief time ("one hour"). Nevertheless, even these minor nations have sided with the beast, receiving power from him and following his lead in the war against the church for however long they have endured.

The Main Event: Lamb *vs*. Beast

But the story does not end with the unbelieving nations finally destroying the people of Christ. The ultimate end to the tale of history turns out to be vastly different from what a casual observer might have imagined: The beast is overcome—by a Lamb!   **17:14**

What assurance and comfort! Despite apparent weakness and seeming defeat and destruction, the church of Jesus emerges from the age-long battle victorious— scarred perhaps, but unbowed. We see again and again in this book that the frightening figures it employs are not intended to *scare*, but to *prepare*. Although the world may afflict the church with its worst torments, fullness of life for all eternity awaits us if we endure in faith and obedience to the end. "Trust and obey, for there's no other way!"

The Self-Destruction of Evil

After describing the beast and what it symbolizes, the angel speaking to John now returns his attention to the harlot. The actual identification of the harlot is left until the end of the chapter, but we are told from   **17:15**

the outset that her influence falls upon all "peoples and
multitudes and nations and tongues." The harlot "sits"
upon the whole world, holding it down under her weight.
It appears that the seductive attractiveness of the harlot and the strength of the beast form an irresistible
combination which controls the earth. But then something strange and quite unexpected happens: The beast
turns against the harlot and destroys her.   **17:16,**

How can this be? We have seen it plainly revealed in   **17**
this vision that the beast and the harlot represent the
evil world-system and its seductive attractiveness to
men. The beast has even been supporting the harlot as
she rode upon it. How can it now destroy her?

Jesus once asked, "If Satan casts out Satan, he is
divided against himself; how then shall his kingdom
stand?" (Matt. 12:26). His question is answered in this
vision. Satan's kingdom, when finally divided, will not
stand. It will crumble beneath the weight of its own
wickedness.

The harlot, representing the allure of the evil world-
system, is carried for a time by the ugly beast. No one
seems to notice the horrible nature of the beast itself,
for all eyes have been drawn to the charms of the harlot. But when the world has been caught up in the spell
of evil, so that there is no turning back, then the beast
has no more need of the seductiveness of the woman. It
devours her. Only then is the beast seen as it really is,
in all of its grotesque and destructive horror.

To put it in more general terms, the attractiveness of
evil sooner or later wears off, and only its brutishness
remains. The Evil One may appear as "an angel of
light" (2 Cor. 11:14), but only to attract the unsuspecting
moths of the unbelieving world. Once they are within
the radius of his heat, he consumes them with fire, and
only too late is his deceptiveness understood.

But in this attack against the seductive harlot, the   **17:18**
beast makes its fatal error. It divides its own kingdom.
Only one outcome can result: the fall of both the "great
city, which reigns over the kings of the earth," and the

final destruction of the Evil One. This ultimate downfall of evil is the subject of the rest of the vision.

Seven Voices of Judgment: Babylon's Destruction

In Revelation 18 and 19 we encounter a full description of the final fall of "Babylon," the antichrist world-
system which has for so long looked to itself for ultimate salvation from all dangers and ills. Like the church
in Laodicea, this city of the unbelieving world has considered itself to be self-sufficient and "in need of noth-   3:17
ing." Consequently, it has never sought the truth and
deliverance that are in Jesus.

You must remember that the Babylon being spoken of
here is not some imaginary, far off, mystical realm. It is
the world *today*, a world which has attempted to throw
off the rule of God. The Revelation speaks here of our
nation, our cities, our neighborhoods.

The catastrophic consequences of living out the antichrist world view, of behaving godlessly, are enumerated
through seven voices which call out to us, describing
from various perspectives the fall of Babylon.

I. The Voice of the Glorious Angel: Babylon's Immorality Condemned

After John's angelic guide has concluded his inter-   18:1
pretation of the meaning of the beast and the harlot,
John sees in his vision another angel. The beauty of
this angel is so great that "the earth was illumined
with his glory."

Notice that this glorious angel appears immediately
following the scene which showed us the gaudiness of
the harlot. Her charms only appeared attractive in the
absence of true beauty. Here, when the glory of this
heavenly being shines forth, the harlot shrivels in her
depravity. This is the way it is with all forms of evil;
they may seem attractive for a time, but when one

glimpses the beauty of God's righteousness, desire for
the sin which once seemed so pleasing fades.

This dazzling angel declares the final fall of Babylon.
The former home of opulence becomes the residence of
unparalleled horror. The great collapse of this city of   18:2
the world is caused by its "immorality" and "sensuality."   18:3
Such language, though sexual in nature, refers to all of
the worldly desires and practices of men for which they
so willingly sell their souls. The "wealth" men derive
from citizenship in this wicked city, whether measured
financially, materially, or sensually, is at best transito-
ry, and it leads to absolute and total poverty for eternity.

II. The Voice Out of Heaven:
The Call to Holiness

A second voice calls from heaven, this one to you and   18:4,5
me. It is the call to sanctification and holiness, exhorting
and warning us to come out from the contamination of
this evil city of the world. When judgment falls in double strength, poured out from the cup of the wrath of
God, we must be far from her. Perhaps the greatest   18:6
tragedy of modern Christendom is its willing participation in Babylonian interests and preoccupations.

I don't have to look too far in my own life to see my
own tendency towards Babylonian values. It's easy for
me to spend more hours reading *Time* and *Sports Il-
lustrated* than studying God's Word. I'm much more
tempted to squander an evening with a basketball game,
Netflix, or Jimmy Fallon than to meet quietly with my
Lord. Could we be running from God? Why do we avoid
Him? Yes, we live in Babylon, and too often Babylon lives
in us.

Opposing our tendency toward worldliness, the voice
of God cries out, "Come out of her. . . ."

Because of the world's puffed-up pride and its depre-   18:8
ciation of any need for the living God, "torment and
mourning" will be poured out upon it, for "the Lord

God who judges her is strong." This latter phrase is a study in understatement. The strength of the world is really weakness, while the rejected God is almighty in His judgment.

The most amazing truth in all of this is that you and I deserve the same horrible judgment which befalls Babylon. It is only the substitutionary death of the Lord Jesus Christ on our behalf which delivers us from being numbered among the citizens of this doomed city.

III. The Voice of Kings: Babylon's Strength Destroyed

The "kings of the earth," signifying those who have been responsible for the continuing dominance of Babylon over the peoples of the world, mourn at the sight of the city's destruction. But they weep for more than the downfall of a system. They weep for themselves. For with the destruction of "the strong city," which seemed to them invincible, comes their own demise. In one swift moment ("one hour") judgment has come, and who is able to stand? **18:9** **18:10**

For many, the sudden personal realization of this doom will come too late. In that hour there will be no more hope for them. This horrible thought should compel you to cry out to your friends, even as God does, "Come out of her, for the hour is near."

IV. The Voice of the Merchants: Babylon's Wealth Destroyed

If there has been one thing which has typified the world-system of Babylon throughout the centuries, it has been the desire for the things of this world. Jesus warned against the dangers of worshipping the god mammon (wealth) and of seeking after treasure on the earth instead of in heaven, but His words have gone largely unheeded (see Matt. 6:20–24). The expensive costume of the harlot and the great wealth which is laid **18:11– 18** waste at the destruction of her city serve to remind us of the foolish futility of this world's materialism.

As believers, we are encouraged by this vision to have an attitude toward material things different from that of Babylon. Since worldly wealth is the security of that great world-encompassing city, panic—as well as pain and despair—run rampant when these possessions **18:19** are laid to waste. "They threw dust on their heads and were crying out, weeping and mourning" because of the destruction of worldly goods. Because these men of the world had not laid up for themselves treasure in heaven, they had no other security. Because we know that it is in Christ's kingdom where true wealth lies, we should be able to rise above earthly loss to receive heavenly gain. Which is your attitude toward *your* possessions, that of Jesus' or Babylon's?

The underlying cause behind this final downfall of **18:20** the materialistic system is revealed next. We are told that it is on behalf of His people, the "saints and apostles and prophets," that God brings about the demise of the church's enemy, Babylon. How unfitting it is for those who *claim* to be among the children of God to flirt with that brazen harlot, by feverishly seeking the things of this world. After all, what does it profit if you gain even the whole world, if in the process you lose, for all eternity, your own soul (see Mark 8:36)?

V. The Voice of the Strong Angel: Babylon's Life Destroyed

After showing the world's despair over Babylon's **18:21** approaching judgment, John tells us that he sees a "strong angel," who signifies the omnipotence of God over all of His creation. This angel reenacts the "throwing down" of Babylon, as he takes up a great stone and hurls it into the sea. As it sinks to the miry bottom, the angel compares the stone's descent to the final sinking of Babylon, which is never to rise again.

In the verses that follow, it becomes plain that all life **18:22** in the wicked city is cut off. Music, usually associated with happiness, will be heard no more. The fine craftsmen of the city will not ply their trades any longer, for there is none to buy or sell. The light of a lamp will not be **18:23** found, for all the city has become darkness. Even the joys of the bride and bridegroom will be turned to wailing. Here is a horrible picture of ultimate death: the experience of the righteous judgment of God, the eternal separation from His blessing, the eternal presence of His curse.

Why is God's judgment so total? It is because Babylon **18:24** has totally rejected God and given themselves to evil, as demonstrated by how they mistreated and murdered His holy ones. The time has come for the avenging of the martyrs' blood. God has waited patiently for all to turn to Him, but now the great day of the Lord has arrived, to bend the knees of those who refused to kneel before Him.

VI. The Voice of the Heavenly Multitude: Praise for Christ's Victory Over Babylon

With the realization that their age-long prayers for **19:1** the destruction of Christ's enemies are being answered at last, the blessed multitude in heaven breaks out in a doxology of praise.

It is important to notice the motive behind this exul- **19:2** tation at the destruction of Babylon. This is not revenge. It is rather a desire to see truth prevail and the righteousness of God vindicated in the earth. Throughout this age the people of God have warned the skeptical world of the approaching judgment, only to see their Lord mocked and rejected. God's patience with such scorners has been great, but now the time comes for Him to demonstrate to these mockers that all they once laughed at is true.

God is praised "because His judgments are true and righteous," and it is right that the harlot is condemned because she "was corrupting the earth with her immorality." It is no low desire to see the enemy "get his" which rouses this cry of praise. It is joy at the vindica-

tion of the holiness of God. Even the ever-billowing   **19:3**
smoke rising from the eternal flames of the harlot's
destruction is cause for rejoicing. It serves as a reminder
of the wages of sin and the justice of God, and also of
His grace which has called some of us out of that destruction into life.

All of the church and all of creation join in this heav-   **19:4**
enly praise, as the twenty-four elders and the four living creatures lift their voices in confirmation of the
multitude's adoration. With the fall of this world-system,
which has plagued the earth throughout the centuries,
the entire watching universe breaks forth with shouts
of gratitude, for that which has long threatened to destroy God's creation has at last itself been destroyed.

The Marriage Supper of the Lamb

The praise from the innumerable heavenly multitude   **19:6**
continues as the Lord's rule over all is at last acknowledged, as every knee bows before Him.

Then comes the announcement that the marriage   **19:7**
feast of the Lamb has been prepared, and His Bride is
about to appear in her spotless beauty. She has been   **19:8**
made ready, being dressed not in the tatters by which
she was known in this world, but in the fine and clean
linen of holiness. Because those dressed in these garments are holy, it is plain that all of those so arrayed   **19:9**
are blessed of God. Sometimes we hear that holy obedience to Christ is not important for those who are to be
saved, but it is evident in this scene that righteousness
is a prerequisite to being clothed in the festal robes of
the wedding of the Lamb.

The Bride, of course, is the church of Jesus in all of
her perfected glory into which she will be transformed
at His coming. But the Bride is selected not because of
her own worthiness, but because she has believed in
the Lord Jesus Christ, and because she has pursued
that sanctification apart from which no one shall see
the Lord (see Heb. 12:14). There is no conflict between
faith and obedience (see James 2:14–26). The true church

is obedient in its faith and faithful in its obedience. Do not ever separate them. Prepare for your part in this heavenly feast.

John is so overcome with this glorious scene that he **19:10** falls at the feet of his heavenly guide and begins to worship him. But he is quickly prevented, for all praise must go solely to the triune God who has accomplished the great events of salvation for those who believe. No creature, however exalted, can hold even a candle to the sunlight of His worthiness. As if to confirm that fact, John looks up and sees the vision to end all visions. He sees the mighty Lord Jesus Christ in His triumphant return.

King of Kings, and Lord of Lords: The End of the World

As he watches the heavens roll back, John beholds a **19:11** mighty war horse with the righteous, faithful, and true One riding upon it. This is the Lord Jesus Christ, the same Lord who once rode humbly into Jerusalem on a donkey. But now He comes in majesty, not in meekness. That first time He came as a rejected Savior; now He comes as a discriminating Judge who does fierce battle with those who have shown themselves to be His enemies.

His very appearance inspires fear. The ruler of heav- **19:12** en and earth is returning to claim His rightful domain, to wrest it from those who have so presumptuously and foolishly sought to usurp it. His victory is sure, for the battle has already been fought and won at the cost of **19:13** His own blood. That shed blood, which seemed for a time to be a sign of His defeat, has become an emblem and means of triumph.

All of this glory afforded Jesus is supremely appropriate, for He is called "The Word of God," that One who was in the beginning with God, and who from the beginning was God (see John 1:1). We who follow after **19:14** Him, the redeemed church He has bought, form His armies. We, too, ride white horses, symbols of victory,

for we are identified with our Lord, being overcomers
through Him.

Since this returning King is The Word of God, it is **19:15**
from His mouth that the sword of judgment flashes
forth. During His earthly ministry, Jesus warned His
foes that it would be His word that would judge them
on the Last Day (see John 12:48). Now the Last Day has
arrived, and His promise is fulfilled. The sword of His
mouth, the Word of God, smites all who have rejected
Him. It is the Lord Jesus Himself who treads the wine **14:19,**
press of judgment described in an earlier vision.   **20**

He first came to save; now He returns to judge (see
John 3:17,27). Those who have not met Him by faith
through His first coming will surely face Him in judgment at His second. He is the One with whom we have
to do, for He is God Himself, the King of kings and the
Lord of lords.

VII. The Call to the Great Supper of God:
The Final Destruction of Christ's Enemies

This "great supper of God" is the second supper **19:17**
mentioned in this vision; how different the two are from
one another! The first was the marriage supper of the
Lamb, where those clothed in the white robes of righteousness were bidden to sit eternally at the Lord's
table with Him. But this second supper is hideous, not
a meal of God's covenant blessing but of His final curse.

Thus far in these visions we have seen the destruction of the temporal worldly kingdom of the Evil One
and those who follow him. The vision now concludes
with a representation of their eternal destruction,
depicted in a scene of rotting flesh and carrion-filled
vultures.

Those being devoured in this last judgment include **19:18**
both the "small and great" of this world, both "free men
and slaves." There need not be a great deal which these
men have shared in common. It is enough that they
had agreed on one thing: The rightful reign of Jesus
Christ over their lives had to be overthrown! Instead of

accomplishing that usurpation, it is they themselves who are thrown over, to the vultures of eternal death.

All of the leaders of the world-system put together, **19:19** including the beast who has empowered them, are un- **19:20** able to oppose Christ's irresistible will. The beast and the false prophet, those forces of evil which have given rise to the antichrist secular and religious systems of the world, are finally destroyed in the everlasting lake of fire.

In the next vision, we will find that all those who **20:15** have followed their leadership in this world will also follow them to a fiery end. Through the imagery of this **19:21** vision, we are shown that the truth of Christ's word ("the sword which came from the mouth of Him who sat upon the horse") serves as His enemies' condemnation, and that the foul birds of curse eat their fill of their flesh.

Living in Babylon

In studying this vision we have contemplated the seductive deception of the harlot Babylon, and we have been warned to stay far from her epicenter of immorality. We have seen the ultimate condemnation and destruction of that harlot, the great and evil system which has been built in the image of man rather than in the image of God. We have been reminded that her prestige and power are only superficial and temporary, and that we, the children of Christ, outcasts from that city of destruction, will ultimately win out.

But in the meantime—until that day of final victory—I beg you to continue to live on the outskirts of Babylon. Even though you are not of the world, you are nevertheless in it. Because this is true, as followers of Jesus Christ we must guard ourselves against the wiles of the worldly harlot

Where is your weakness? Where do you fear that you could fall? As we begin the twenty-first century,

Babylon is exerting its power more than in all of previous history. The harlot's seductions are more tantalizing than ever. Be armed with persevering faith, holiness, and the gospel of the crucified and risen Christ. Boldly continue your warfare against the world, wielding the sword of the Spirit, the Word of God (see Eph. 6:13–17).

Resist Babylon with confidence. Even though you are badly outnumbered, Jesus has promised that the gates of hell shall not stand against the onslaught of His church (see Matt 16:18). Onward, Christian soldier. Your **2:10** King calls you to battle! Be faithful until death, and He will give you the crown of life.

9. Meet Your Maker

Revelation 20 presents a vision of Christ's victory over Satan at the Cross. Then it quickly moves through all of history to the final judgment, when Satan and death are at last destroyed. During this entire span of history, as believers in Christ we are not only preserved; we are pictured in the vision as reigning with Christ in the heavens.

The Binding of Satan

The chapter opens with a representation of the most **20:1–3** significant event of history: the victory of Jesus Christ over the power of the Evil One, which He accomplished through His death on the Cross. His resurrection from the dead, His ascension into heaven, and His reigning at the right hand of the Father complete His saving work. This complex of redemptive acts brings about the eternal salvation of all of us for whom Christ performed them, and it simultaneously spells the defeat of Satan.

This victory is signified by the vision of the binding of Satan, which John describes. Satan (a spiritual being) is bound by an angel (also a spiritual being) and its effects are felt in the spiritual world.

Satan was bound through the power of Christ's death and resurrection, and he continues to be chained wherever the truth of the gospel frees men from the Evil One's lies. But this kind of talk almost always brings up the query, Why is there still evil in the world? If

Satan has been bound, shouldn't sin already be eradicated from the earth?

That is a fair question, and it is answered with a careful reading of our text. We are told that Satan is bound for one specific purpose: "so that he should not deceive the nations any longer." We naturally tend to think in physical terms. If a person is bound, he is incapable of any activity at all. But remember that Satan is spiritually bound, which does not necessarily render him impotent in every area. He is said to be bound specifically from one type of action, "from deceiving the nations any longer." Let's find out what that restriction actually means.

Before the coming of Jesus the Messiah, the only people on the face of the earth who had open and free access to the one true God were the Israelites, the people of God's covenant. From time to time a non-Jew, or Gentile, would be grafted in to the nation of Israel through belief in Jehovah, but by and large the Gentile world lay in total spiritual darkness. All of the Gentile nations were under the control of Satan, as he deceived them into sinfully worshipping man-made gods and even man himself. The non-Israelite who did wish to know the living God had to go to Jerusalem, where God made Himself accessible to His people in the temple.

But with the coming of Jesus and His work of redemption, everything changed. The command of God was no longer for the world to come to Jerusalem to find God. Now Jesus' instruction to his followers was to start in Jerusalem and go to the uttermost parts of the earth, so that men might know God regardless of where they live or the background from which they come (see Matt. 28:18–20).

The church of Jesus Christ is now present amidst every nation, tongue, and tribe. Satan is bound from deceiving Gentile nations any longer.

In Matthew 12:29 and Mark 3:27, Jesus describes His binding of Satan in graphic terms. He envisions the whole world as Satan's "house," over which Satan, the "strong man," has exercised control for a long time. Jesus describes Himself as one who wishes to break into that house and carry off the "property" in it, the people who have been under the darkness of the Evil One's household. So Jesus asks, "How can anyone enter the strong man's house and carry off his property, unless he first binds the strong man? And then he will plunder his house."

From the earliest days following the crucifixion, people from every nation have been responding to the message of the Cross and coming to Christ by the thousands and millions. Jesus is carrying off the property which once belonged to Satan. But according to Jesus' own words, He could not do this unless the strong man had been bound. Satan was bound from deceiving the nations through the Cross of Christ, and he is so bound today.

But why then is there still unbelief and disobedience? There are still many people who do not trust in the gospel of Christ, and these men and women remain blinded by the Devil. Although there are individuals who do not believe, it is no longer the case that whole nations are prevented from hearing and believing the truth. We have already discovered that the 144,000 includes people from every nation, and all peoples and tongues and tribes. The strong man has thus been bound, and Jesus through His ambassadors continues to carry off Satan's goods, rescuing the Devil's prisoners from the kingdom of darkness and bringing them into His kingdom of light.

The Thousand Years

Christians often wonder about the seemingly mysterious period of time in the twentieth chapter of the Revelation called "a thousand years." The Latin rendering of the phrase "thousand years" has given us the

20:2, 4,6

English word *millennium*, the term by which this period is most commonly known. What is this Millennium, and when does it occur?

The first thing we should examine in answering those questions is the number *one thousand*. We have already noticed that the Book of Revelation is rich in numerical imagery: the fours, sevens, tens, twelves, twenty-fours, the 666, and the 144,000 are obviously all symbolic rather than statistical. The number one thousand is used here to signify a particular truth—but what?

When we were studying the meaning of the 144,000, we found that one thousand is used to express a wholeness or completeness. He owns "the cattle on a thousand hills" (Ps. 50:10) means "He owns all the cattle." In the same way, the thousand years represents the wholeness or completeness of the time that God is using to carry out His perfect plan for this world. The thousand years in the vision represents God's entire program as it is unfolded in history, from the first coming of Jesus to His return.

There are at least two ways to confirm this interpretation. One we have already examined. We have seen that the primary characteristic of the Millennium is the binding of Satan; that binding was accomplished by Jesus on the Cross. Since Satan is "bound . . . for a thousand years," a binding that began with the Cross and continues to the present day, the thousand years of Revelation 20 is that same period of time. We are now in that Millennium, the time of Satan's restraint from deceiving the Gentiles.

The Reign of the Saints With Christ

The second aspect of the Millennium mentioned in Revelation 20 is the reign of the saints (or true believers) with Christ through the church age, called "a thousand years." If we can discern when this rule occurs, again we will have an indicator of the presence and duration of the Millennium.

First of all, note that the reign of Christ spoken of in Revelation 20 is not an earthly reign but a heavenly one. There is nothing in this passage to suggest that Jesus reigns from an earthly throne. The idea of an earthly reign is contrary to the words of Jesus Himself when He said, "My kingdom is not of this world" (John 18:36).

The unbelieving Jews at the time of Christ were looking for the establishment of an earthly kingdom by the Messiah, and Jesus refuted that mistaken notion. As believers, we should not make the same error by looking for a material, worldly kingdom of Christ. Jesus' rule is in the realm of the heavenlies, as He indicated at His ascension when He said that "all authority...in heaven and on earth" had been given to Him (Matt. 28:18). He had not won a worldly, military victory but a spiritual triumph in the Resurrection.

Those who reign with Him participate in this spiritual rule. These "vice-monarchs" reign in the heavenly rather than the earthly world, for they themselves are spirits, the souls of saints who have died in the faith and who are now with Christ in heaven. There are two categories of these souls made perfect:

1) Those who have been beheaded.

2) Those who have not worshipped the beast or received his mark.

The first category represents a special mention of all those who have been martyred for their faith, with the second group including all other Christians who have died, remaining faithful unto the end. Although to the present world they seem to be dead, in heaven they are alive to reign with Christ during this present age. What a comfort it is to tired and beleaguered Christians to know that our labor on this earth is not in vain. We will live again to rule with the King of kings and Lord of lords!

The Scripture speaks of three stages in our Christian

experience which are related to life and death. The first is in this world, where we are "at home in the body [but] absent from the Lord" (2 Cor. 5:6). The second is after physical death, when we are "absent from the body and...at home with the Lord" (2 Cor. 5:8). The third and final stage follows the resurrection of believers at the end of the age, when, after receiving our new resurrection bodies, we are both at home in the body and at home with the Lord.

The souls reigning with Christ in Revelation 20 are in the second of these three stages, being in heaven with Christ, but still without physical bodies. This means that the time of their ruling with Christ precedes the resurrection of believers and is therefore in the present age. Your loved ones who have died in the Lord are at this very moment with Christ singing praises to Him, participating in His glorious heavenly reign and awaiting the end of the age.

This is the second indicator, then, that the thousand years is not future but present. We are now in the Millennium and have been since the ascension of Jesus to the right hand of God, when His heavenly reign as God and man began.

The First Resurrection

Following John's description of departed believers in **20:5** heaven with Christ, we are told in a parenthetical comment that "the rest of the dead did not come to life until the thousand years were completed." "The rest of the dead" refers to those who die in rebellious rejection of Christ and who therefore are not in heaven. They are unseen from the heavenly perspective. Though they continue to exist even after physical death, they are not alive in the spiritual sense, but dead. At the end of the thousand years when Jesus returns to judge the world, they will come to life in the resurrection of their bodies to give an account. Then they must face the final judgment without Christ to defend them from the justice of God. How blessed are we who know that Jesus is our Advocate, our defense attorney, and that we will overcome because of His payment of the penalty for our sin.

After this explanatory note, John begins to speak of **20:6** something called "the first resurrection." Those who have "a part" in the first resurrection are said to be "blessed and holy." The second death, the lake of fire, has no power over them, and as priests of God and Christ they will reign with him for a thousand years.

Some have suggested that perhaps the "first resurrection" refers to the quickening to spiritual life which comes when one is born again by the Spirit of God. This is a possible interpretation, but it faces the difficulty that in the New Testament the word *resurrection* seems always to refer to a physical rather than only a spiritual vivification.

It is certainly true that, while we were dead in our sins, we were brought to life through faith in Christ. But if proper use of *resurrection* indicates the dead coming to life in the physical sense, then what is the first resurrection? The answer is so obvious it is easily missed.

The first resurrection is the bodily resurrection of Jesus from the tomb. His was the first resurrection of One who is never to die again. (The raisings of Lazarus and the others in the New Testament were not resurrections in this same sense, for those people came to life for a time but then died again.) Jesus' is the first resurrection to eternal life in the new glorified body. On the Last Day all believers will be likewise resurrected and united with "resurrection bodies" (see John 6:39, 40). This "Last Day resurrection" of all men could be called the "second resurrection," while Jesus' resurrection was the first.

If Jesus' was the first resurrection, in what sense can others be said to have a part in it? And who are those who have a part? Paul writes in Ephesians 2 that those who are "in Christ" are identified with Him in every way. "Even when we were dead in our transgressions,

[God] made us alive together with Christ (by grace you have been saved), and raised us up with Him, and seated us with Him in the heavenly places, in Christ Jesus" (vv. 5,6).

This means that God considers us to be in such vital union with the resurrected Christ that we are already raised from the dead, already ruling with Him. The world may consider you and me to be of no significance whatsoever, but for Jesus' sake the Father has counted us worthy to sit with His Son on His throne in the heavenly places. We are each a beloved child of God, loved even as Jesus is. (Now, what was it you were depressed about?)

Those who have a part in the first resurrection are called in this passage "blessed and holy." To whom does John refer here? Of course, it is those of us united to Christ by faith. Who are the ones over whom "the second death has no power"? Again, it is you and I who believe, who have overcome the fear of hell through Christ. Who are those who are "priests of God and of Christ"? Those of us who share in the priesthood of believers with all of the people of Christ (see 1 Pet. 2:5,9). And who reigns with Christ for the thousand years? Again, it is we who have overcome the evil of this world through Jesus.

In other words, this age in which we now live is:

1) The time of the reign of the saints with Christ.

2) The time during which we as believers have a part in His resurrection.

3) The period during which Satan is bound from deceiving the nations.

Since these three characteristics encompass the Scriptures' only descriptions of the Millennium (Revelation 20 is the only chapter of the Bible which specifically mentions the thousand years), our conclusion is confirmed. The Millennium is not sometime in the future. It is now. The next great event on the calendar of God is the return of Christ, the end of the world, and the resurrection of all men for the judgment of the Last Day.

As people to whom I minister have embraced this truth, they have felt a renewed urgency to share the good news of Jesus with their family and friends. There is no second chance, so we must work while it is light, for the night is coming when no man can work. Today is the day of salvation.

The Release of Satan

Following this interlude describing the reign of believers and the first resurrection, John returns to his discussion of what will befall Satan. We have seen him bound through the Cross of Christ, and perhaps we should expect that to be the last we hear of him. But it is not. We are told that "when the thousand years are completed, Satan will be released from his prison, and will come out to deceive the nations...." **20:7,8**

What did we see earlier that Satan was specifically bound from doing? "Deceiving the nations." What do we find him doing immediately upon his release? "Deceiving the nations." Satan always does what he does best. Apparently his deceptive activities are his most developed, as they had their start long ago in the Garden of Eden when the serpent deceived Eve. At the end of the thousand years, he is "released for a short time," **20:3** and he quickly gets his worldwide deception back into action.

When we studied Revelation 11 we learned the significance of the two witnesses in the midst of the great city. We saw that they represented the church, preaching in the midst of a hostile world. We read there that "when they have finished their testimony, the beast **11:7** that comes up out of the abyss will make war with them, and overcome them and kill them." That beast coming up out of the abyss is another way of describing Satan being "released from his prison" to make war **20:9** against "the camp of the saints and the beloved city," the church.

Revelation 11 describes the battle for spiritual supremacy in this world from one perspective and Revelation 20 from another. Nevertheless, both predict the resurgence of satanic influence as we near the end of history. Both teach that there will be an apparent defeat of the church, but that ultimately the final victory will belong to Christ and His people, the overcomers.

The Final Battle

As we learned in our previous study of the final battle of Armageddon, John is not describing an earthly, military war. The final battle is a spiritual conflict fought between the forces of light and the armies of darkness.

It is Satan who gathers together the evil combatants **20:8** in this final spiritual battle. These armies of the Evil One are identified as "the nations which are in the four corners of the earth, Gog and Magog." In the prophecy of Ezekiel, Gog and Magog are names which are applied to the enemies of Israel (see Ezek. 38:2). Here, however, they designate not merely one or two nations, but the nations which are in the four corners of the earth. In other words, Gog and Magog have become names signifying the whole unbelieving world as it comes under the deceptive influence of Satan. Through his deceit there will be a more intense hatred of the church than ever before in history.

Certainly the church universal is under attack from the world today in a way which is unprecedented. Perhaps you have experienced, as I have, spiritual, verbal, and even physical attack because of your faith. Whether or not this indicates that Satan has already been released and that therefore the time of the end is very near, we cannot absolutely determine. But in any case, we who are the church in America and around the world need to equip ourselves for the spiritual battle which already surrounds us. It is sure to intensify. Most Christian soldiers are totally out of shape, ill-equipped to go "marching as to war." It is time to undergo a spiritual rearmament, so that we can learn to wield the sword of the Spirit, the Word of God, as it is intended to be used.

The final gathering together of all of the spiritually wicked forces of the world against the church appears to be the end for the people of God. But at the critical moment, when it seems that the witness and power of the church have been snuffed out at last, God intervenes by bringing about the final destruction of His enemies, signified by the "fire [coming] down from heav-   **20:9** en and [devouring] them."

The White Throne Judgment

The enemies of Christ are dealt with in two stages of   **20:10** judgment. First, the spiritually wicked forces behind the world's animosity toward Christ and His church (represented by the Devil, the beast, and the false prophet), are tormented forever and ever in the lake of fire. Second, the men and women who have throughout history opposed Christ are brought before the judgment seat of God, the "great white throne," where they stand   **20:11** alongside the believers whom they have persecuted. God is upon His throne. Imagine the terror of those who have scorned ideas of His existence, mocked His Word, and refused His offer of forgiveness in Christ as they stand face to face with this God whom they have denied.

There are two types of books which shall be opened: **20:12** the "books of deeds" and the "book of life." All the dead are to be judged according to what is found in the books. Every person is judged according to his deeds. The fatal   **20:13** problem with this judgment from man's perspective is that no one's deeds are good enough for him to merit the right to enter into eternal life. As Jesus said, "You are to be perfect, as your heavenly Father is perfect" (Matt. 5:48). It is plain that not one of us meets that standard. Because "all have sinned" (Rom. 3:23) and "the wages of sin is death" (Rom. 6:23),

all alike stand condemned before the justice of God.
But there is an incredible hope.

If one's name is found in the Book of Life, the record   **20:15**
of those who have come into true life by trusting in
Jesus, he is counted as having the sinlessness and the
righteousness of Christ. Thus he is considered to be
perfect and qualified to enter in to the presence of the
all-holy God. But "if anyone's name was not found in
the book of life, he was thrown into the lake of fire."

This brings the crux of your eternity down to this
question: What is your relationship with Jesus? Will
you be found serving Christ in His body the church?

The Death of Death

Finally, we are told that "death and Hades were thrown   **20:14**
into the lake of fire." As Paul writes in his letter to the
Corinthians, the last enemy to be destroyed is death (1
Cor. 15:26). At the close of this present age, with its
characteristic corruption and rebellion against God, sin
itself will come to an end. Transgression originally
entered the world through the rebellion of Adam against
the Word of God, and sin has continued down through
history as we sinful children of Adam have carried on
his disobedience. But when sin is finished, so is death,
for "the wages of sin is death." And if death is done
away, then Hades, the abode of the dead, has no further
use either. Enter: the lake of fire.

At the end of the world, all men will be in one of two
conditions: They will be in the presence of God, a blessing which has been earned for them by the life and
death of Jesus. Or they will be in the lake of fire, the
terrible eternal curse of God, which they themselves
have earned. This is the state of which Jesus spoke
when He said, "Where their worm does not die and the
fire is not quenched" (Mark 9:48).

Everyone will spend forever somewhere. God has giv-
en us a choice of two abodes.

10. Forever Yours

Eternity.

Who hasn't at one time or another pondered the meaning of the word. Everything in this creation has had a beginning. But what about the end?

The Word of God tells us that those who believe in Jesus have eternal life. We have become so accustomed to hearing that phrase that it has become almost a cliche; it does not instill within us the incredible awe that it should. But think about it. As the great hymn proclaims,

> *When we've been there*
> *Ten thousand years,*
> *Bright shining as the sun,*
> *We've no less days*
> *To sing God's praise*
> *Than when we'd first begun.*

None of us can really know what that means until we get there.

Nonetheless, the final two chapters of the Revelation afford us a holy glimpse into the glories of the eternal world which Jesus has gone before us to prepare. As with the other visions in the book, these images of that future world represent realities too magnificent for human language to express.

The New World Coming

Chapter 21 opens with John's vision of the new creation God will bring about following His destruction of the present world.

The first verse of this chapter is reminiscent of the   **21:1**
opening words of the Bible: "In the beginning God created the heavens and the earth" (Gen. 1:1). That was the beginning of the present cosmos, one which has fallen under the effects of sin and which thus must be destroyed. But here in the Revelation we have a *new* beginning, a re-creation of a world where sin, sorrow, pain, and death will be unknown.

There are a number of unexpected characteristics of this new world which are revealed to us. For example, in the new creation, "there is no longer any sea." This at first seems to be a rather strange comment, until we remember what the sea represents. You will recall that the seven-headed beast of chapter 13 came up "out of   **13:1**
the sea," and that the harlot of chapter 17 "sits on   **17:15**
many waters." We are told that these waters represent the "peoples and multitudes and nations and tongues" of this evil world-system in which we now live.

By pointing out there is no sea in the new creation, John emphasizes from the very beginning of this vision that the sin and human turmoil of this present age will be eradicated from the world to come.

The City From the Sky

The first thing John sees in the new creation is "the   **21:2**
holy city, new Jerusalem, coming down out of heaven from God. . . ." A city coming down out of the sky? What could this mean? Remember that John is speaking of a revelation which has come to him through a vision. The correct question is: What does this "new Jerusalem" from the sky represent? Fortunately, the chapter we

are studying gives us the answer to this question.

In verse 9 an angel tells John that he is about to **21:9**
show him "the bride, the wife of the Lamb." We know
from other Scripture that the "bride of Christ" is the
church (see Eph. 5:23–27). We who are united to Jesus
by faith are called His "bride" or wife. In other words,
when the angel tells John that he is going to show him
the bride of Christ in all her glory, he is speaking of the
church of Jesus.

In the next verse John recounts that the angel takes **21:10**
him away and shows him "the holy city, Jerusalem."
The angel tells John that he will show him the church,
but then he shows him what John calls "Jerusalem."

The Jerusalem of which John speaks is the church of
Christ, finally come to its perfection in the new age. In
Old Testament times God chose Jerusalem as His earthly dwelling place, where He could be approached by His
people through sacrifice. Since the time of Christ, however, the whole new creation has become the Jerusalem
where the Holy Spirit dwells, where Christ's people
live, and where they have constant access to God. This
access is opened to us not because of our own limited
sacrifices, but because of Jesus' infinite offering on the
Cross.

This is what we are told by the voice from the throne **21:3**
which cries out, "the [God] shall dwell among them, and
they shall be His people. . . ." Someday, perhaps soon,
you, as a believer in Christ, will actually be in the
presence of God Himself. Therefore, you will be wise in
this world to prepare yourself to meet Him and to dwell
forever with Him, as well as with other believers. You
might as well learn to get along with your brothers and
sisters now—you'll be spending eternity together!

The Fullness of Joy

When you finally find yourself in the presence of **21:4**
your heavenly Father, as awesome as the thought may

be, you will experience total joy. There will be no more "mourning, or crying, or pain." The tears left from earth's sorrows, God Himself will wipe from your eyes. Here is the ultimate fulfillment of calling upon God as your Father. As a loving father tenderly cares for his precious children, so God provides for your most intimate needs. The providential care which you experience in this world is but a small foretaste of the richness of His love, love which will be yours forever through Jesus.

Next we hear a voice coming out of the throne itself **21:5** speaking of the re-creation and renovation of all things. This is the voice of God from His throne, as He proclaims His accomplishment of the fullness of the new creation.

It is noteworthy that this voice from the throne of **21:6** God says, "I am the Alpha and the Omega, the beginning and the end." This is important because in the next chapter we hear Jesus saying exactly the same thing of Himself: "I am the Alpha and the Omega . . . the beginning **22:13** and the end." As we have seen before, John very clearly teaches throughout this book that while the Persons of God the Father, God the Son, (and God the Holy Spirit) may be properly distinguished one from the other, still we have one God, with all these Persons sharing fully the same divine nature and attributes. Jesus, the Alpha and Omega, is at once God and man forever, the One who paid the penalty for our sins and who has prepared a place for us in Paradise.

Promises and Warnings

A voice from the throne calls out promises of bless- **21:6–8** ings and pronouncements of curses, comforting words and also unsettling words. These words are meant for us today to hear and heed. The free gift of "the water of life," the gospel which leads to eternal life, is offered to all who thirst for it. Anyone who asks for this water will receive it, and that without cost; Jesus has already paid for it.

New life and all the mysterious wonders of the new creation belong to those who do not succumb to the evil of the present age but who overcome evil through Christ's victory. On the other hand, those who reject God's free offer of life, those whose very lives demonstrate that their home is not heaven, will find their end in the lake of fire, where the Devil and those who have followed his rebellion are tormented forever.

This horrible message of the lake of fire represents an attempt to explain something which is frightening beyond words. A momentary brush against a hot stove can bring about pain that lasts for days. But try to imagine an entire lake of fire, and that you are thrown into its flames. Even more terrible, imagine that although you burn, you cannot die so as to stop the pain. This is the terrible imagery which the Scripture uses to describe the eternal curse of God.

Whatever it is that awaits those who mock and shun the work of Christ for sinners, it is more terrible than any mortal can dream. This is no scare tactic. It is the Word of God, and that Word presents a warning to those who take lightly the message of the Scriptures. This warning is an act of God's grace and love. He has told the unrepentant in advance what awaits them, so that they might turn from their sin to Christ and escape the judgment to come (see 2 Pet. 3:9).

A Guided Tour of New Jerusalem

Following these promises and warnings, our attention is turned to a dazzling description of the new Jerusalem, the church of Jesus Christ, now come into its perfection in the new age. John begins to describe for us the beauty and brilliance of this heavenly city which has come down to the new earth.   **21:11**

With regard to the new Jerusalem, note the use of the number *twelve* over and over again in its description. There are first of all twelve gates into the city,   **21:12**

with twelve angels to guard them. This reminds us of
the truth that only those who have come via the way of
the Son ("no one comes to the Father, but through Me"
[John 14:6]) are allowed to enter in. On each of the gates
of the city is one of the names of "the twelve tribes of
the sons of Israel." Moreover, the city is said to have   **21:14**
twelve foundation stones, each of which bears one of the
"twelve names of the twelve apostles of the Lamb."

This combination of the tribes of Old Testament Israel and the names of the New Testament apostles depicts the unity of the people of God throughout time,
whether before or after Christ. The believers of the Old
Testament trusted that God would send a Deliverer to
bear away their sins; we believers of this present age
trust that God *has* sent Him. But all are saved by faith
in the Savior sent by the Father into the world. Thus it
is appropriate that the one eternal city described here
should be built upon the foundation of the leaders from
both the Old and New Testament congregations.

Next, the city is measured in John's presence by the   **21:15,**
angel speaking with him. We discover here something   **16**
rather curious about the city. Not only is it laid out as a
square, but "its length and width and height are equal."
This means, of course, that the city has the shape of a
cube. What could possibly be the significance of this?

The New Holy of Holies

In 1 Kings we are given the layout and dimensions of
the temple built by Solomon in Jerusalem. From the
description of the Holy of Holies we learn that its dimensions were 20 cubits by 20 cubits by 20 cubits (1
Kin. 6:20). In other words, the Holy of Holies was cubi-
cal in shape, its length and width and height being
equal.

This Holy of Holies was the special covenant dwelling place of God among His people. Because it was the
most sacred spot on the face of the earth, sinful men

were not allowed to enter into it. Only on the annual Yom Kippur, the Day of Atonement, was the High Priest allowed to purify himself and then enter in to make atonement on behalf of the people of Israel. This was a solemn and terrifying moment for that priest, for the presence of the holy God is an awesome thing.

Yet, in the new Jerusalem which John describes, the **21:16** whole city is a cube, with God dwelling in the midst of it. The entire city is the new Holy of Holies. But instead of falling back in terror at the thought of entering in to that place, as the men of old did, we *live* there. Because we have received by faith the very holiness and righteousness of Christ, we shall walk freely in the presence of God in the world to come. Total acceptance and perfect righteousness are what we inherit from the Lord Jesus.

The Meaning of the Wall

As the angel measures the city, he tells John the **21:17** dimensions of the wall surrounding it. (At this point some translations of the Bible do a very poor job of communicating what was intended by these figures. Instead of giving us the Greek units of dimension for the wall, some translators have converted the ancient measurements of *stadia* and *cubits* into modern miles, yards, and feet. In so doing, these translators have totally missed the point.)

The Greek text tells us that the wall's length (and height) around the city is "twelve thousand stadia," and that its thickness is "one hundred forty-four cubits." It is futile to turn to conversion tables to figure out the distances in modern units of measure. Again, I repeat: These numbers are symbols, not statistics, and it is plain what they mean.

This city is so identified with the church that its very dimensions are revelatory of that fact. Once again twelve and its multiple are utilized as the numbers representing the people of God. This eternal city is prepared especially for us who have overcome through faith in Jesus.

The Opulence of the City

The cities of the ancient world were, as are many metropolitan areas today, rather dirty and dingy places. Though there were glimpses here and there of magnificence, the shabbiness of every city was evident. But the new Jerusalem which God is preparing for you and me offers quite a contrast.

That new city is "pure gold"; even "the street of the city [is] pure gold." We make our cities out of concrete and our streets out of asphalt. Gold is reserved for use in setting precious gems and as a standard of currency; it is the most valuable of this world's treasures. But in the age to come life is so abundant and the splendor of God so magnificent that gold is used to pave the paths under our feet. **21:18, 21**

The foundation of the city is seen as being composed of gigantic precious stones, twelve of them bearing the names of the twelve apostles, the foundation upon which Paul tells us the church has been built (see Eph. 2:20). And the gates of the city, which bear the names of the twelve tribes of Israel, are enormous pearls, indicating that those who enter therein have given all they have to obtain the pearl of great price, the kingdom of God (see Matt. 13:45,46). **21:19, 20**

The Seven Missing Things

Although this magnificent new Jerusalem is more glorious than human mind can absorb, there are some things which will be missing. In the vision of chapters 21 and 22 we are told of seven things which, although they are present in this world, will be absent from the world to come.

We have already looked at two of those seven. (I)   **21:1**
There will be "no sea," meaning that the evil and turmoil of this present age will be done away, and (II)
neither will there be any "mourning, or crying, or pain,"   **21:4**
representing the total absence of the miseries of this
world which will be enjoyed in the world to come.

III. No Temple

In the latter half of chapter 21 we read of four more   **21:22**
things specifically said to be missing from the next
world. John says, "I saw no temple in it |the new city|,
for the Lord God, the Almighty, and the Lamb, are its
temple."

We have already learned how the temple represented
the local presence of God, where He was approachable
for those who sought to worship Him. As a structure it
was considered to be much more important than what
we think of today as a church building, for in a very
true sense it was "the house of God."

But we read that in the new creation there is no
longer the need for a temple. There is no need for a
particular location to represent man's ability to approach
his Creator. God the Father and His Son, the Lamb, are
the temple. The presence of the Lord is immediately
available to all who have come to Him.

As Christians, we experience even in this world a
taste of that immediacy of communication through worship, prayer, the hearing of His Word, and by the presence of His Spirit within and among us. But in the
eternal days to come we shall see Him face to face and
know Him even as He now knows us.

IV. No Sun or Moon

Not only will the temple be unnecessary in the New   **21:23**
Jerusalem, but there is no need for the luminaries of
the heavens, the sun and the moon. In the first Creation, God made the sun and the moon to give light to
the earth. But in the new creation this need for light
will be met in another way. The sun and moon are the

givers of physical light to this material world, and so
they become apt contrasts to the source of true light,
Jesus Christ Himself.

The Scriptures authored by John are rich in the imagery of light and darkness. Most specifically, John writes
that "God is light, and in Him there is no darkness at
all" (1 John 1:5), and "The light is come into the world,
and men loved the darkness rather than the light; for
their deeds were evil" (John 3:19). Jesus Himself said,
"I am the light of the world" (John 8:12). In these met-
aphors, sin and Satan are represented by darkness,
and God's power and righteousness by light. In that
world there will be no need for solar or lunar illumina-
tion because the holiness of the Father and the Son will
light the city. The righteousness of Christ will fill the
land, and the glory of the Lord will cover the earth.

God intends for your life to be shining forth that
light of His holiness even today, for we believers are,
along with Christ, "the light of the world" (Matt. 5:14).
Just as darkness is defined as the absence of light, so
wickedness arises in the absence of Christ's Spirit in
one's life. But as one small candle dispels the darkness,
so even a simple faith can credit the righteousness of
Jesus to your heavenly account.

V. No Night

The absence of sun and moon is closely related to the   **21:25,**
next of the seven missing things, expressed in the phrase,   **26**
"there shall be no night there." Darkness is a metaphor
for evil; thus, in the New Jerusalem it will never be
dark. There will be no unholy thing which survives the
final cataclysm of this age so as to enter in to the new
world. There will be perpetual peace and righteousness,
signified by the omnipresence of light and the total
absence of darkness.

VI. No Unclean Thing

The imagery of light with no darkness in turn leads   **21:27**
to the sixth missing thing. There shall be "nothing

unclean and no one who practices abomination and lying"
in that bright city. The twelve angels guarding its gates
will protect its perpetually open doors from the entrance
of those who have not been made worthy by the blood of
the Lamb. "Only those whose names are written in the
Lamb's book of life" will enter in. If one is truly a possessor of eternal life, he will not be a practicer of abomination, lying, and the host of other activities not befit-
ting the child of God.

We who have eternal life know that we are not saved
by good works, but we are not saved without them either. The writer to the Hebrews reminds us that we
must pursue "the sanctification without which no one
will see the Lord" (Heb. 12:14). As you rejoice in the
absolutely free gift of eternal life, you must not allow
your freedom to turn into license. Your Lord has called
you to be holy, even as He is. Those who continue in sin
are showing the world the true nature of their hearts—
regardless of what they may say, they are not children
of the Father, heirs of eternal life.

VII. No More Curse

The seventh and final missing thing is revealed in   22:3
chapter 22, where we find that "there shall no longer
be any curse." This removal of the curse is especially
significant, for it reminds us of the overriding problem
which has caused those things missing in the world to
come to be present in the current age.

Because of the curse on this world, there is the turmoil among the nations of the earth. Because of the
curse, there is crying, pain, and death. Because of the
curse, there was need for a temple where man could
approach God, even in his sin. Because of the curse
there has been spiritual darkness, necessitating artifi-
cial attempts at producing light. Because of the curse,
this world is filled with those who openly practice their
rebellion against Jesus Christ and who hate His people.

But when we read that there shall no longer be any

curse, we know that with that one truth all of the effects of sin will be removed, and the pristine righteousness of God over the human race will be restored.

This passage concerning the removal of the curse of **22:2** sin is found in a context which is laced with imagery from the Genesis account of the Garden of Eden (see Gen. 3). Access to "the tree of life" which once grew in the midst of the Garden (and which would have bestowed eternal life upon Adam and Eve) is no longer forbidden in the new earth. In fact, the tree holds a central place in the new Jerusalem and bears twelve kinds of fruit twelve times a year.

Here is a marvelous picture of life abundant and ev- **22:1** erlasting: The tree of life is nourished by "a river of the water of life." Life this concentrated and this fruitful is unknown to mortals of this world, but it shall be the daily experience of us all when the curse of sin is removed forever.

It was in the Garden of Eden that the curse was originally leveled against man and woman because of their disobedience to the plain commandment of God. Before that fall from perfect righteousness, the man and woman related openly and freely to their Creator. But when the spiritual death of the curse fell upon them, the face of God was hidden from them and was replaced with the curse. The human troubles which have plagued mankind throughout time, including all the difficulties you face today, have arisen from that original rebellion and curse. But when the curse is re- **22:4** moved, we "shall see His face," and that fellowship broken so long ago shall at last be totally restored.

The Seven Final Words

The prophecy of the Revelation closes with the account of seven different witnesses who testify to the truth of the prophecy of this book and who call those who hear the prophecy to come to faith. This entreaty

sounds forth to you and me and to all men, that we
might become partakers in its promised blessings rather
than its threatened curses.

I. The Testimony of the Father

We have noted from the very beginning of this study   22:6
that this Book of Revelation claims to be no less than
the Word of God Himself. God has revealed the visions
of this book for the good of His people. To be sure, He
mediated them through His angel to John, and thus to
us. But they are no less the direct revelations of God.
John emphasizes that the same Holy Spirit which inspired the prophets has led him into these visions; the
words he has written are "faithful and true," even as
God Himself is. You can bet your life on them.

II. The Testimony of John

Following an interlude when the words of Jesus con-   22:7
cerning His return echo through John's mind, John
presents his own witness to the veracity of his prophecy. John puts his reputation on the line, as it were,   22:8
when he says, "I, John, am the one who heard and saw
these things." This is no unsigned, anonymous prophecy. John is willing to stake his standing as an apostle of
Jesus Christ upon the truthfulness of the visions he
has reported. This was serious business, for John was
well acquainted with the punishment for those who
spoke falsehood in the name of the Lord—the death
penalty (see Deut. 18:20).

John, in fact, is so overwhelmed at what he has been
shown that he falls a second time to worship at the feet
of the angel who has opened the visions to him. The
angel reminds John (and us as well) that it is God alone
who deserves worship. This makes all the more striking the fact that throughout the scenes of the Revelation, the Lamb Jesus has received the worship of saints
and of angels. Not once was anyone reproved for so
revering Him. Conclusion: Jesus Christ is God.

Thus John's testimony is not only to the truthfulness

of the visions which he has recorded. It also attests the veracity of Jesus' claim to be of one nature with His Father (see John 10:30).

III. The Testimony of the Angel

The angel with whom John has been speaking in this **22:9** vision now adds his own words to the affirmation of the Revelation's truth. He stresses the fact that he is only a fellow servant of John and the prophets. Then he adds that he is also a fellow servant with those who heed the words of the prophecy of this book. In other words, the angel is attesting that those who, like John and the other prophets, really wish to serve God must take this book as the truth of God for the present age.

Next, the angel exhorts John to publish the Revela- **22:10** tion: "Do not seal up the words of the prophecy of this book," but spread them abroad. This book is not written merely for those of the final generation of history. No, indeed. The message of the Revelation was as vital to the first century believers as it is to us, and so John is commanded to get the message out to them as soon as possible. The comforts and encouragements for the church (and the warnings to her enemies) were just as relevant and crucial then as they are today. Even then it could be truly said, "The time is near." If the end was near then, what must we say of our own generation?

Verse 11 fixes men and women into their eternal **22:11** conditions. The point is that there will be no time to change one's ways after Jesus comes back. The "one who is filthy" will remain filthy for eternity, and "the one who is holy" will dwell among the holy ones forever and ever.

This is a warning to all those who say, "Oh, I'll wait until later to accept Christ. In the meantime, I've got a lot of living to do." There are two mistakes in such an attitude. The first is that none of us is guaranteed a "later" in life. Today may be the day of His coming, at which time eternity, either in heaven or in hell, will begin for all men.

The second error involved in such a statement is that it assumes that a person can come to Christ any time he wishes. But Jesus has said, "No one can come to Me unless it has been granted him from the Father" (John 6:65). No man should forget the exhortation, "Today if you hear His voice, do not harden your hearts" (Heb. 4:7). And Christian, do not be deceived into resting your hope for eternal life on an "experience" you may have had years ago. If the Lord is not real to you today, you need to get right with Him *now*.

IV. The Testimony of Jesus

The words of Jesus follow the testimony of the angel.   **22:12**
He speaks not only of His return, but of the fact that "My reward is with Me, to render to every man according to what he has done." The word "reward" in this verse really means "wage." In other words, whatever a person has earned as his wage, whether good or bad, will be meted out on that day. And this judgment will befall "every man."

Jesus alone has the authority to pass such judgment   **22:13**
because He is "the Alpha and the Omega, the first and the last, the beginning and the end." As we have seen before, these appellations identify Jesus Christ as God, the One to whom all judgment belongs. He is the One through whom the world was created (John 1:3)—the beginning—and He is the One through whom it will come to its close—the end. As such, Jesus deserves and demands everyone's adoration, including yours and mine.

Because of who Jesus is, those who "wash their robes"   **22:14**
in His sacrificial blood inherit the right to eat of the tree of life and to enter into the eternal city. Adam, because of his sin, was denied access to the tree of life. The second Adam, Jesus Christ, because of His righteousness, has earned the right to eat of it on behalf of all those who trust and depend upon Him alone. Those who have not had the robes of their lives washed in His blood remain outside the gates, in the outer darkness.

The six types of men described here are typical of those **22:15**
who have remained uncleansed and thus unforgiven.

Finally, Jesus sets His seal upon the words of this **22:16**
Book of Revelation. It was His angel who brought these
words to us, and He Himself says that the truths, comforts, encouragements, and warnings of the Revelation
are for the benefit of the churches. Again we see the
immediate relevance of the message of this book to our
first-century brothers and sisters. It is a terrible mis-
take to relegate the bulk of the message of the Revelation to the terminal generation living in the last few
years before His return, when it has been intended as a
blessing to all generations.

As the "root and the offspring of David," Jesus identifies
Himself as both the Creator who brought David into
being and as the Messiah who was a descendant of the
lineage of David. As "the bright morning star" Jesus
points to the dawning of a new day which His coming
signals, the unending day of eternity.

V, VI, VII. The Testimony of the Spirit, the Bride, and the One Who Hears

The witness of the final three of the seven testimonies
is actually a unison invitation from all three to you, the
reader of the Revelation. This invitation is made up of
one significant word: "Come."

First, the Spirit says, "Come." The Holy Spirit is al- **22:17**
ways the initiator of the new birth when one comes to
Christ. From the human perspective we say that a man
or woman "decides to accept Christ," and this is true.
But we must not forget the unseen work of the Spirit
who has gone before, to prepare our hearts to hear the
message of the gospel and to enable us to believe. The
invitation of the Spirit is mandatory if we are to come
to Him in faith.

But amazingly, the invitation of the Holy Spirit does
not stand alone. His call is accompanied by the invitation of "the bride." The bride, of course, is the church,
including you and me. Notice that the invitation of the

church repeats the word of the Holy Spirit, and yet her invitation is necessary. God has ordained that the hearing of the gospel be the instrument by which men come to saving faith, for "how shall they believe in Him whom they have not heard?" (Rom. 10:14). It is the duty of the church, of you and me, to make sure that our message is the same as that of the Spirit, and that we make provision to bear that message to the world. It might be difficult for you to think of winning the whole world, but you can speak to your neighbor, your sister-in-law, and your employer. That is where your world begins.

This encouragement is emphasized as "the one who hears" says "Come." Ultimately we individual believers who have heard the truth of the gospel, who have been brought to life through it, must be the vessels carrying the invitation of the Holy Spirit and the church. If you have truly believed you will desire to do this very thing. The one who is content to go to heaven without others is probably not going there himself. We who possess the Holy Spirit of God will most certainly be interested in the welfare of those who may be headed for a Christless eternity.

The Book's Final Warning

So crucial and relevant to the church of all eras are **22:18,19** the words of this book of prophecy that a solemn warning is given to those who would tamper with it. Nothing must be added; nothing omitted. The full counsel of God must be proclaimed to His people. To be sure, much of this Book of Revelation is difficult to understand, but those who seek by the Spirit to grasp its meaning shall understand that which is needful. After all, it is not the Book of Concealment, but the Book of Revelation. It is intended by God to bless and comfort all those who read it and heed it.

We hear the words of Jesus, "Yes, I am coming quick- **22:20** ly," and we pray with John, "Amen. Come Lord Jesus."

The Last Word

We began this book with the hope that we could find in the Revelation comfort and encouragement for these difficult days in which we live.

We have found that God cares for us so much that He has revealed Himself in a book (the Bible) and in a Person (Jesus Christ) so that we might know Him intimately.

We have been both rebuked and encouraged by the admonitions and commendations afforded the seven churches of first-century Asia Minor—for we have seen that conditions in our churches today are much like theirs.

We have learned that apparent weakness often disguises true strength, and that "when we are weak, then we are strong"—for the Lord is our help in time of trouble.

We have been comforted by the truth that the Lord will preserve us who belong to Jesus, even in the midst of the world's dissolution.

We have been warned, however, that those who continue in self-ruling rebellion against their Creator will be confronted, not with Christ's blessing, but with His curse.

We have been sobered by the realization that this world groans under the sway of the beastly systems of humanistic secularism and false religion, but we have rejoiced with the knowledge that the dragon and his beasts are doomed to final defeat at the hand of Christ.

We have been lifted up by learning that someday evil itself will die and that Jesus has gone ahead of us to prepare a place for His own which is beyond our ability to comprehend, a home where life and light cast out all death and darkness.

Finally, we have discovered that regardless of our disappointments in life, despite our weaknesses and trials, we are overcomers through Jesus Christ. We are victorious because He has won the eternal victory for us. On the last page of the Bible there is no sin, no death, and no devil. None of these things will survive the end of this world—but you will. Why? Because you belong to Christ; you are an overcomer. As He Himself reminds you in John 16:33, " 'In the world you have tribulation, but take courage; I have overcome the world.' "

GLOSSARY

This is a glossary containing summaries of the meanings of some of the major figurative images found in the Revelation. They are listed chronologically, according to the chapter and verse. Each definition is followed by a number in parentheses, indicating the chapter in this book where further discussion of the symbols may be found.

Revelation 1

The seven Spirits who are before the throne: The Holy   **1:4**
Spirit in His sevenfold ministry to the church. (1)
The seven lampstands: The seven churches whom   **1:12**
Christ addresses in chapters 2 and 3. (1)
The seven stars: The "messengers" or overseers of the   **1:16**
seven churches of the Revelation. (1)

Revelation 2

The Nicolaitans: Followers of a first-century heresy   **2:6**
which taught that one could be a Christian and still
be regularly involved in idolatry, immorality, and compromise with the antichrist world-system. (2)
The synagogue of Satan: Jews in the first century   **2:9**
were among the strongest persecutors of the early
church. They thought themselves to be members of
the synagogue of Jehovah, but by seeking the downfall of the church they showed themselves to be mem-

bers of the synagogue of Satan, the accuser of the
brethren. (2)

Tribulation for ten days: A figurative way of describ- **2:10**
ing a comparatively brief period of persecution. Though
brief in duration, this affliction of the church accomplished the purposes for which God brought it about
(indicated by the number ten, signifying completeness).
(2)

The teaching of Balaam: The false doctrine that one **2:14**
can worship both God and idols, that he can immerse
himself in the ways of the world and yet be a true
follower of Christ. (2)

The hidden manna: Heavenly food representing spiri- **2:17**
tual sustenance, accessible at the Lord's table to the
"overcomers." Jesus called Himself the heavenly manna, the bread of life. (2)

The white stone: An ancient sign of innocence in a **2:17**
law court, representing the legal acquittal of the believer because of Christ's atonement. (2)

The teaching of Jezebel: Like that of the Nicolaitans, **2:20**
a teaching which encouraged compromise of the faith
with the evil practices of the world. (2)   **2:28**

The morning star: An ancient symbol of royalty, a
royalty belonging to Christ and shared by His peo-   **22:16**
ple. Jesus calls Himself "the bright morning star." (2,
10)

Revelation 3

White garments: Representations of the righteousness **3:5**
imputed to believers in Christ because of His perfect
holiness. (2)

The Book of Life: Ancient cities kept records of those **3:5**
who lived within the city. When a person was born,
his name was written in the book, and when he died,
it was erased. Believers' names will not be erased
from God's Book of Life, for they will never die. (2)

The key of David: Representative of the right to grant **3:7**

or deny entrance into the Heavenly Jerusalem. This
key is held by Jesus. (2)

Those who dwell upon the earth: A phrase used   **3:10**
throughout the entire Book of Revelation to represent the unbelieving world in contrast with the church.

Revelation 4

The throne in heaven: A figure of the sovereign rule   **4:2**
of God over all His creation. (3)

The rainbow around the throne: Like the rainbow   **4:3**
God gave to Noah, which was a symbol of God's covenant to preserve the world and those who love Him.
(3)

The twenty-four elders: Representatives of the church   **4:4**
of Christ in its presence before the Lord. The number
twenty-four is the sum of twelve plus twelve, twelve
being the number of the church in both the Old and
New Testaments. (3)

The four living creatures: Beings which represent all   **4:6,7**
of creation as it rightly worships and serves its Creator. *Four* is generally acknowledged to be the number
of creation. (3)

Revelation 5

The sealed book: A book which symbolizes God's plan   **5:1**
of redemption of His people and the destruction of
His enemies, as revealed in the seven seals which are
subsequently opened by the Lamb. (3)

The Lion of Judah: The symbol of the royal strength   **5:5**
of the Messiah, unexpectedly revealed in the form of
a Lamb, normally considered a weak and gentle creature. (3)

The Lamb: A figurative image of Jesus Christ, the   **5:6**

Lamb of God, the perfect sacrifice for sin, who takes away the sins of the world. (3)

Seven horns: A symbol of perfect strength, the Lamb's   **5:6**
omnipotence. (3)

Seven eyes: A symbol of perfect knowledge, the Lamb's   **5:6**
omniscience. Both the omnipotence and omniscience
of the Lamb indicate His divinity. (3)

The new song: The song which is sung by the twenty-   **5:9**
four elders (representing the church) extolling the
Lamb for giving His life for His flock; thus it is the
message of the gospel of Jesus Christ. (3)

Revelation 6

The white horse: A figure of man's insatiable desire   **6:2**
to rule over his fellow man, a rule accomplished by
conquest. (4)

The red horse: A signification of the bloodshed and   **6:4**
killing which accompanies man's selfish ambitions
to assert himself over others. (4)

The black horse: A picture of the economic turmoil   **6:5**
which is everpresent in a world which refuses to live
according to the precepts of God. (4)

The pale horse: A representation of the various forms   **6:8**
of unexpected death which befall men in this present
age. Life is uncertain for those who depend solely
upon themselves, rather than upon God, for their
sustenance. (4)

The souls under the altar in heaven: Believers in Christ   **6:9**
who have been martyred because of their faith, who
now look forward to the day of judgment when their
blood will be avenged. (4)

The cataclysmic events of the sixth seal: Earth-   **6:12–14**
shattering events which indicate the end of this present age and prepare the way for the new creation of
the world to come. (4)

The seven types of men fleeing from the Lamb: Fig-   **6:15** ures which represent all of the types of people on the earth, from kings to slaves. Regardless of worldly station, all must stand together before the judgment of God. (4)

Revelation 7

The four angels at the corners of the earth: Angels   **7:1**
which signify the withholding of the wrath of God from those who are about to be sealed, that is, His church. (4)

The 144,000: The number which is the figurative   **7:4**
representation of the church, composed of all those who have trusted in the Deliverer sent by the Father, regardless of the time or place in which they have lived. (4)

Every tribe of the sons of Israel: The true Israel, the   **7:4**
church, the real offspring of Abraham through faith in Messiah Jesus. (4)

The great multitude: The representation of the church   **7:9**
which John sees after hearing the number 144,000 which is identified with them. (4)

The great tribulation: The tribulation of the church   **7:14**
has been continuously present since the church's inception and will increase at the end. The world-system, led by the Evil One, is constantly battling and attempting to exterminate the true people of Christ, just as it tried to kill Jesus. (4)

Revelation 8

The silence of the seventh seal: The eternal peace of   **8:1**
the new creation which follows the sealing of the people of Christ and the destruction of this present world. (4)

The first four trumpets: Trumpets figuratively as-   **8:6–12**

sociated with the plagues which fell upon Egypt in
the time of Moses, they describe the displeasure of
God with the evil world which subjugates His people
today. (5)

The eagle flying in midheaven: A more accurate trans-   8:13
lation of "eagle" would be "vulture." Because of the
judgments which fall with the final three trumpets,
this bird of carnage cries out his warning to the unbelieving world. (5)

Revelation 9

The star fallen from heaven to earth: Satan, who was   9:1
cast out of heaven and granted the key to the abyss
in order to unleash the judgment of God upon the
world. (5)

The locusts from the bottomless pit: Figures depicting   9:3
the displeasure of God with the wicked earth and His
judgment which shall consume it. The eerie description of the locusts comes from the prophecy of Joel, as
he foretells the coming of the Day of the Lord. (5)

The five months of torment: A reference to the 150   9:5
days (or five months) during which the waters of the
Flood covered the earth as a judgment against unbelievers; here indicating a worldwide judgment in our
day as well. (5)

The angels bound at the river Euphrates: A represen-   9:14
tation of the way in which the world-system is destroyed. The angels do not attack the church but the
unbelieving world as part of God's general judgment
against sin. (5)

The two hundred million horsemen: Not a statistic,   9:16
but an image of the tremendous power and effect of
the plague upon the earth that arises from the blowing of the sixth trumpet; again representing God's
judgment against unbelief. (5)

Revelation 10

The little book: A book which, open and in the hand **10:2**
of the strong angel, represents the Word of God in its
worldwide significance. (5)

The seven peals of thunder: The meaning of these **10:3,4**
thunder peals is unknown. (5)

Revelation 11

The temple of God: A signification of the church, as **11:1**
compared with the "court outside the temple" which
has been given to the nations; the latter represents
the antichrist world outside the church. (5)

The forty-two months (see also "twelve hundred and **11:2**
sixty days" and "a time and times and half a time"):
The entire time period between the first and second
comings of Christ. It is the time during which the
church is persecuted by the world, the time of the
prophesying of the two witnesses to the world, the
time of the woman's protection and nourishment in
the wilderness, and the time of the authority of the
sea-beast. All of these symbols span the entire present age in their meanings.

The two witnesses: The believing church in its role as **11:3**
witness to the hostile world. As the church, the
witnesses are invincible against the most severe attacks of the world. The church may seem to be overcome, but it will finally emerge victorious on the last
day as it is vindicated in the presence of its enemies.
(5)

The twelve hundred and sixty days: The entire time **11:3**
period between the first and second comings of Christ.
(See "forty-two months" above.) (5)

The great city called Sodom and Egypt. The antichrist **11:8**
world-system which is hostile toward God and His
church. Just as Sodom was the place of sin and Egypt

the place of bondage, so the great worldly city holds
in chains of sin the peoples of the earth. It was this
city and its citizenry which necessitated and brought
about the crucifixion of Jesus. (5)

The time for the dead to be judged. The final judg-   **11:18**
ment of all humanity at the end of the world. (5)

Revelation 12

The woman with child: The Old Testament Church,   **12:1,2**
about to give birth to the long awaited Messiah. (6)

The great dragon: Satan and his power for evil. (6)   **12:3**

The seven heads and ten horns: The absolute influ-   **12:3**
ence toward evil and against Christ which the Evil
One exercises in the world. (6)

The male child born to the woman: The Christchild   **12:5**
who accomplishes His given task and returns to heav-
en. (6)

The woman in the wilderness: The church in its cur-   **12:6**
rent state, between the land of bondage to sin and
the promised land of heaven. Israel wandered in the
wilderness for forty-two years, so the church here is
pictured as being in the wilderness forty-two months.
(6)

The twelve hundred and sixty days: See under chap-   **12:6**
ter 11 above.

A time and times and half a time: A time period   **12:14**
equivalent to the forty-two months or twelve hundred
sixty days, all of which are figurative of the interadvent
period. (6)

Revelation 13

The beast from the sea: The satanically-inspired, hu-   **13:1**
manistic world view which attempts to give meaning
to the world without reference to Jesus Christ. This
man-centered system has characterized this entire

age since the birth of Christ and it will continue to do so until the end of time. (6)

The beast's fatal wound which is healed: That blow **13:3** which Satan and his world-system suffered because of Christ's triumph on the Cross. The apparent healing is figurative of the continuance of the beast's influence in the present age, though his time is short. (6)

The forty-two months: See under chapter 11 above. **13:5** (6)

The beast from the earth: The false religious systems of the earth which seek to satisfy man's religious yearnings while always turning him away from the truth which is in Jesus. (6)

The mark of the beast: A spiritual rather than a physi- **13:11** cal mark which indicates that its possessor is owned by the beast and the system he represents. (6)

666: The number representing the culmination of **13:16** man's efforts to replace the authority of God with his own. Six is the number of man, and 666, a trinity of sixes, indicates sinful man's ultimate desire for self-deification and the casting down of the true God and His Son Jesus Christ. (6)

Revelation 14

Mount Zion: Not the earthly mountain which may be **14:1** touched but the heavenly Jerusalem, the true abode of the Lamb and His people. (6)

The 144,000: See under chapter 7 above. (6) **14:1**

Babylon the great: Another name for the antichrist **14:8** world-system which now is in control but which will be decimated at the return of Christ. (6)

The Son of Man with the crown and the sickle: Christ **14:14** at His second coming, preparing for the final judgment of the world. (6)

Revelation 15

The seven bowls full of the wrath of God: Parallel to **15:7**
those of the seals and the trumpets, plagues which
are characteristic of the judgment of God upon this
present evil age. Like the other series of plagues, the
bowls culminate in the day of judgment at the end of
the world. (7)

Revelation 16

The kings from the east: Like the "kings of the whole   **16:12**
world" of the same passage, representatives of demon-
ically inspired attacks against the church, evident
throughout the age, which will increase in intensity
as the end approaches. (7)

The war at Har-Magedon (Armageddon): Represen- **16:16**
tative of the climax of the spiritual battle which has
been waged between the Christless system of the world
and the church of Christ all during this present age.
It is not a military battle but a spiritual one; for our
battle is not against flesh and blood, but against the
dark spiritual forces of evil. (7)

The seventh bowl: Signifies the events immediately **16:17**
accompanying the end of the world and the return of
Christ. (7)

Revelation 17

The great harlot: Babylon, the symbol of the anti- **17:1**
christ world-system, especially in its love of riches.
The world has prostituted itself to gain fleeting plea-
sures rather than eternal ones. (8)

The woman on the scarlet beast: The harlot being **17:3**
supported by the beast, indicating the seductiveness

of the evil world-system which covers the true ugliness of the beast, until it is too late. (8)

The seven kings: Representatives of seven world empires which have held sway at various times throughout history. We are now in the seventh kingdom, the culmination of all of the others in its hatred of the true God and the lifting up of man as the absolute. (8) **17:10**

The ten kings: Representative of all of the short-lived worldly kingdoms which have come and gone since the fall of Rome. Their reign is but for "one hour," a brief and comparatively insignificant amount of time. (8) **17:12**

The ten horns and the beast destroying the harlot: Though the harlot is supported by the beast for a time, he turns on her at last. Here is the self-destructive nature of evil, as one form turns against another. The seductiveness of riches (the harlot) will inevitably bring ruin, often of the self-imposed kind. (8) **17:16**

Revelation 18

Babylon the great: See above, under chapter 14 and "the great harlot" under chapter 17. (8) **18:2**

Revelation 19

The bride of the Lamb: The church made holy and righteous by the life and death of the Lamb, who is coming to take her to Himself and to the celebration of the marriage supper. (8) **19:7**

The One riding the white horse: Jesus at His return, coming in love for His bride and in judgment for the world. (8) **19:11**

The great supper of God: A figure of the final judgment, given in terms of carnage from which vultures pick carrion. (8) **19:17**

The lake of fire: The final place of torment for all of those who have loved the beast and have therefore hated Jesus Christ. (8)   **19:20**

Revelation 20

The binding of Satan from deceiving the nations: A spiritual binding which took place at the Cross and which opened up the nations, heretofore totally deceived by the wiles of the devil, to hear and receive the Gospel. In this sense Satan has been bound throughout the gospel age, for the Word has gone into all the world. (9)   **20:2,3**

The thousand years: The period of history during which God's complete plan for the church and the world are being carried out. The thousand years are identified by the binding of Satan and the reign of the saints with Christ. All of these factors indicate that the thousand years represents this present age, from the first coming of Christ to His return. (9)   **20:2**

The first resurrection: The resurrection of Christ, in which all believers in Him have a part. (9)   **20:5**

Satan released from his prison: For a short period immediately preceding the end of the world, Satan will again be freed to deceive the nations, and the church will be sorely attacked in spiritual battle. (9)   **20:7**

Gog and Magog: Old Testament names for the peoples of the world in their united hatred of Christ and His people, who do spiritual battle against the church. (9)   **20:8**

The camp of the saints and the beloved city: Names for the church, especially as it is undergoing the final spiritual attacks upon it by the satanic system of the world. (9)   **20:9**

The great white throne: The judgment seat of God, representing the arrival of the Last Day, the day of judgment. (9)   **20:11**

The second death: Eternal death, separation from the blessing of God forever, signified by the lake of fire. (9)   **20:14**

Revelation 21

The new heaven and earth: The destruction of the old   **21:1**
world and its order calls for the creation of a new one
where no evil remains. (10)

The holy city, new Jerusalem: The church in its total-   **21:2**
ly redeemed state, finally complete and pure in the
new creation. The bride, the wife of the Lamb, the
church, is the holy city Jerusalem. (10)

The dimensions of the new Jerusalem: Like the Holy   **21:16,**
of Holies, the new Jerusalem is symbolically repre-   **17**
sented as being a perfect cube in shape with dimensions of twelve in every direction. It is the perfectly
prepared dwelling place of the church, whose number is twelve. (10)

No night there: Throughout the Scriptures, darkness   **21:25**
is a symbol of evil. In the new Jerusalem, there is
said to be no darkness or night, representing the fact
that no trace of evil will be found there. (10)

Revelation 22

The water of life: Jesus said to believe in Him was to   **22:1**
drink of "living water." The river of this water in the
center of the new Jerusalem indicates that life there
is dependent upon faith in Jesus Christ. (10)

The tree of life: In the Garden of Eden, Adam and Eve   **22:2**
were barred from eating from this source of eternal
life. In the new garden all will have free access to it,
a figure of the free gift of eternal life all there will
share. (10)

The Spirit and the bride say, "Come": The Holy Spirit   **22:17**
speaks today personally through His Word, the Bi-
ble, and through the bride, His church, calling men
and women to come to Christ. The invitation is given
for all to come and receive the free gift of eternal life,
paid for by the death of Christ on behalf of all who
will believe. (10)

Made in the USA
Middletown, DE
19 August 2023

36979742R00116